HISTORY *of* OTOSCOPY

Author
Joseph B. Touma, M.D.

Co-Author
Adam Van Horn, M.D.

Introduction
John W. House, M.D.

Contributor
B. Joseph Touma, M.D.

Photography
Greg Mencotti

Touma Publishing
Huntington, West Virginia

2019

Book design and layout by
Designs on You!
(designs-on-you.net)

TABLE of CONTENTS

Dedication 4

Foreword 5

Introduction 7

Chapter 1 Specula 9

Chapter 2 Illumination 23

Chapter 3 Magnification 44

Chapter 4 Pre-electric Otoscopes 49

Chapter 5 Electric Otoscopes 62

Chapter 6 Pneumatic Otoscopes 92

Chapter 7 Ear Cleaning and Syringes 101

Chapter 8 Otoscopes with Various Attachments 109

Chapter 9 Pioneers in Otoscopy and Historic Books 114

Footnotes 145

DEDICATION

This book is dedicated to the brilliant inventors chronicled in these pages. They were highly intelligent, curious, focused, and motivated. They had no access to even the Industrial Revolution technology; yet over several hundred years, building on each other's knowledge and breakthroughs, they were able to solve the difficulties of visualization, lighting, and magnification of the tympanic membrane that had eluded everyone since ancient history. With sharp focus, they inspired each other to see and understand what lies in the obscure ear canal. With ingenuity, courage, and dedication, they built the foundation of modern otology.

Joseph B. Touma, M.D.
Author

Adam Van Horn, M.D.
Co-Author

FOREWORD

It is an honor to write the forward for this volume. Joseph Touma, M.D., has the most fascinating collection of medical instruments that includes an in-depth assemblage of otic specula as well as illumination and magnification devices. Even though he does not cover ear trumpets in this book, he has the largest and most comprehensive collection of these early hearing aids. It was my pleasure to visit the Touma ENT Museum in Huntington, West Virginia; I was left speechless by the depth of his wonderful collections. Not only does the Touma ENT Museum have a broad collection of ear specula, otoscopes, and microscopes, but the museum also exhibits an antique pharmacy and early 19th-century ENT offices with original instruments, chairs, and drills.

We in otolaryngology examine the ear daily and take for granted the specula and illumination that we frequently use. As you read this remarkable book, you will learn that many have preceded us in the development of examining tools, allowing us to better help our patients. In this book, Dr. Touma gives us a wonderful look at the advancement of the speculum and illumination dating back to ancient times.

In addition to the detailed descriptions of the instruments, he has carefully illustrated these with photographs from his own collection. As I read this manuscript I was struck by his research and passion for the history of the evolution of these commonly used tools. As a history buff and having an interest in the progress of otosclerosis surgery, it is amazing to think that these innovative surgeons in the late 1800s were operating on the stapes with primitive illumination and specula of their own design.

This book is a must read for all students of medicine and particularly those training to be otologic surgeons.

John W. House, M.D.

House Clinic

Los Angeles, California

INTRODUCTION

· ·

In the present day, when literature in every Protean shape and form has compassed the land, and knowledge may be truly said to run to and fro throughout the earth; and when the polyglot cyclopaedia of the press has outstripped in the race all other feats of human prowess of the nineteenth century, it might be deemed unnecessary to follow the old school system of detailing the early history of that particular branch of the healing art, or its elementary or collateral sciences, of which this essay treats, were it not that in an art but just emerging from the darkness, ignorance, empiricism, prejudice, and superstition, which is even yet the condition of aural medicine and surgery, its history not only becomes interesting, but practically instructive.

— Sir William Wilde

The history of otology can be traced to the ancient civilizations. The same can be said for otoscopy, as one cannot divorce the study of the ear and its pathology from visualization. Except for the speculum, which may have been used to examine the concavity of the ear canal during those earliest times, the fabricated tools of otoscopy are relatively young. This project is an attempt to chronicle the development of these tools and give credit to those who made them possible.

While current literature has addressed the development of instruments such as the ear speculum and the head mirror, to our knowledge the most recent work that gives a fairly complete account of otoscopy is Hans Key-Aberg's *Historical Review of Instruments Used in Otoscopy, Together with a Description of a Method for Photographing the Membrana Tympani*, published in 1919. Key-Aberg was a Swedish otolaryngologist who also served as an army surgeon in Belgrade and Vienna. We are indebted to his review, information from which appears several times in our own text. Without it, the undertaking of this project would have been much more daunting.

In addition to Key-Aberg's work, we consulted the Touma Medical Museum's vast collection of texts by greats such as Sir William Wilde, Joseph Toynbee, and Adam Politzer — as well as more contemporary authors — to guide our understanding of this subject. The museum's collection of otoscopes, specula, and various other devices also afforded us an appreciation for the practical nature of otoscopy's progression. The intent of this book is to provide access to these same resources through text and photographs so that readers may also appreciate the development of otoscopy. Perhaps with an understanding of what was accomplished to land us where we are today, one can conceptualize the direction the field will take in the future.

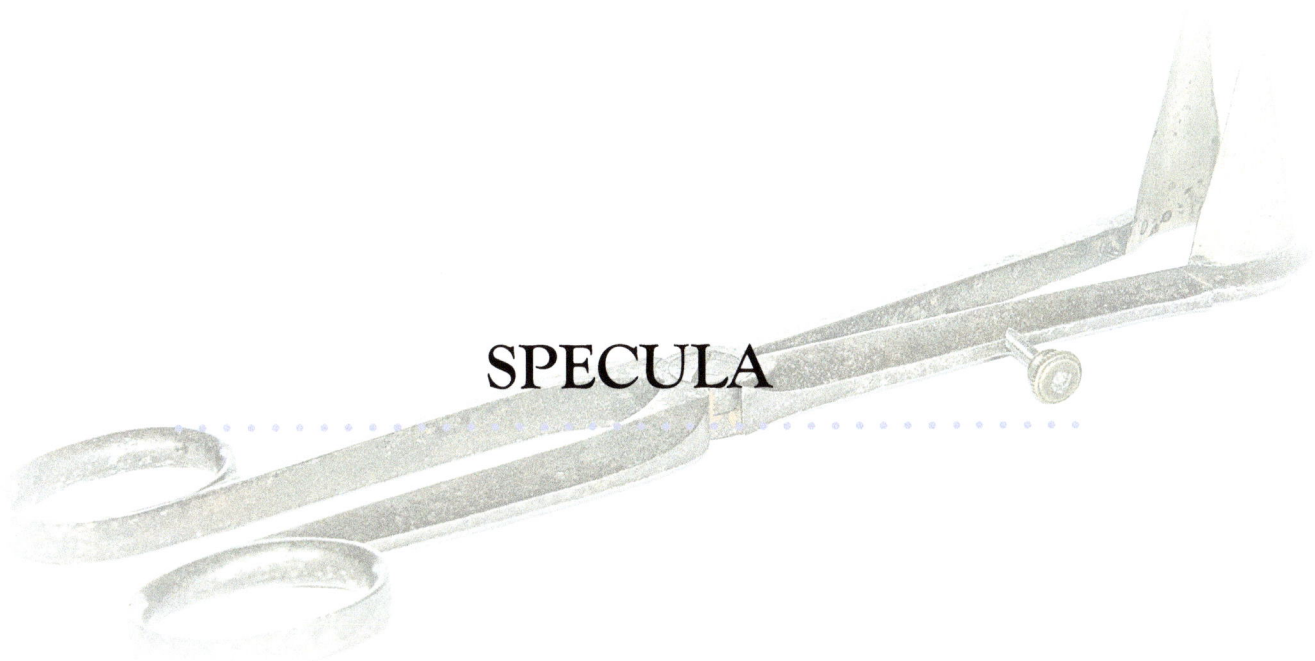

SPECULA

"According to [Thomas] Buchanan," writes Adam Politzer in *History of Otology*, "the auditory meatus is 1¼ to 1½ inches long. At first it courses anteriorly and superiorly, then posteriorly and medially, and finally, inferiorly; anteriorly and medially, it narrows until it reaches a position about one line from the drum where it widens again."[1]

Whether or not Thomas Buchanan's tedious measurements are entirely accurate or widely uniform is certainly debatable. However, the 19th-century English otologist's observation does illustrate how unwelcoming the ear canal is to unaided visual inspection — especially if one wants to see to the terminal tympanic membrane. Difficulty visualizing details of one of the body's concavities is not unique to otology; the use of tools such as a speculum to visualize these cavities dates back to early human civilization. Specula presumably used for medical purposes have been found at ancient archeological sites like Pompeii.[2]

According to Politzer, French surgeon Guy de Chauliac may have been the first to use a speculum to dilate the ear canal: "Chauliac is considered to have been the most ingenious surgeon of the 14th century [and] the most celebrated medical author of the Middle Ages," he writes.[3] While Chauliac undoubtedly suggests the use of an aural speculum in his *Chirugia magna Guidonis de Chauliaco* (1363), many authors attribute the first documented fabrication and use of a designated ear speculum to Fabricius Hildanus, also known as Fabry of Hilden, one of the most respected German surgeons of the 17th century. Similar to today's nasal speculum, his *speculum auris* was a bivalve design with two long, tapering,

Fabricius Hildanus, 17th century German surgeon, described his use of the speculum by reporting on a case in which he **removed a pea-sized glass ball** from the ear of a young girl. According to his report, the ball had been **lodged there for eight years.**

semi-circular arms that could be introduced into the ear canal and then separated by bringing the handles toward one another, thereby dilating the canal. Sir William Wilde dates this design to Hildanus' 1646 publication, *Opera Omnia*.[4] Hildanus described his use of the speculum by reporting on a case in which he removed a pea-sized glass ball from the ear of a young girl. According to his report, the ball had been lodged there for eight years, eluding

the skills of four previous surgeons.[5] Hildanus made no mention of the tympanic membrane in his writings, however, suggesting that the speculum was used only to dilate the meatus.

By the next century, Conrad von Solingen and Jean-Jacques Perret developed their own specula. These were very similar to Hildanus' design — a split, tapering cylinder that would separate for dilation of the ear canal. Not very impressed by these efforts, Key-Aberg

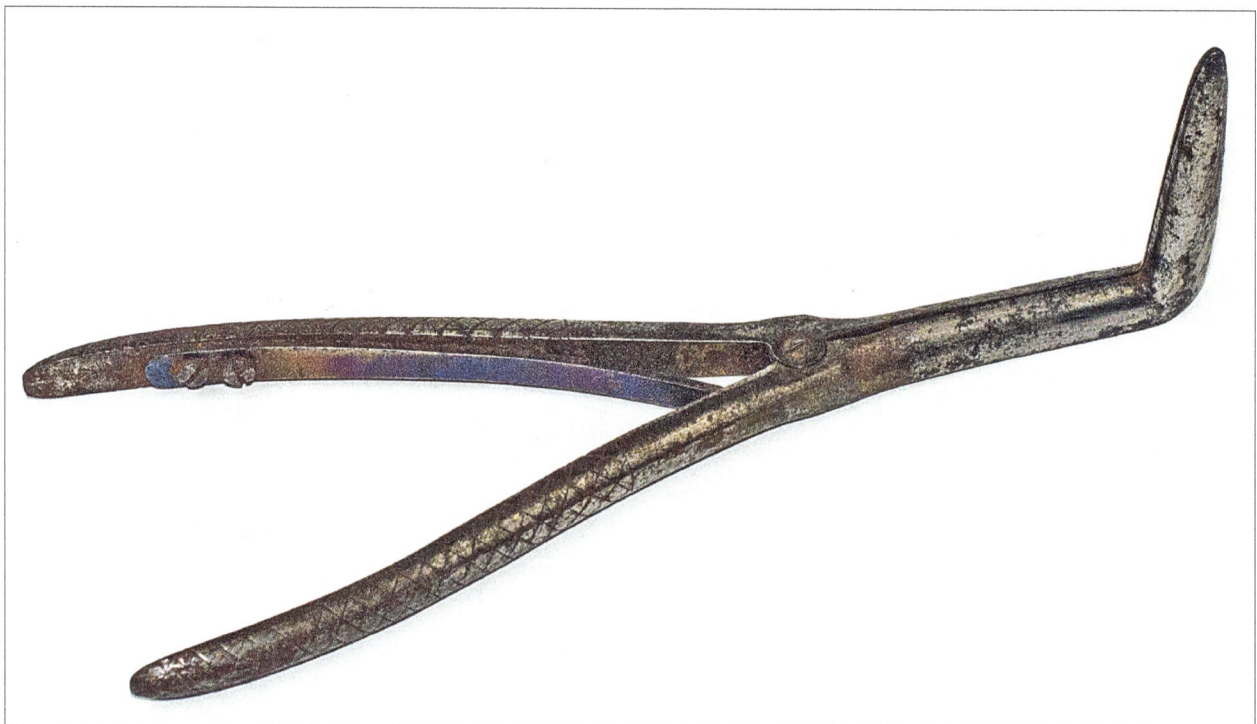

Perret's aural speculum (late 18th century).

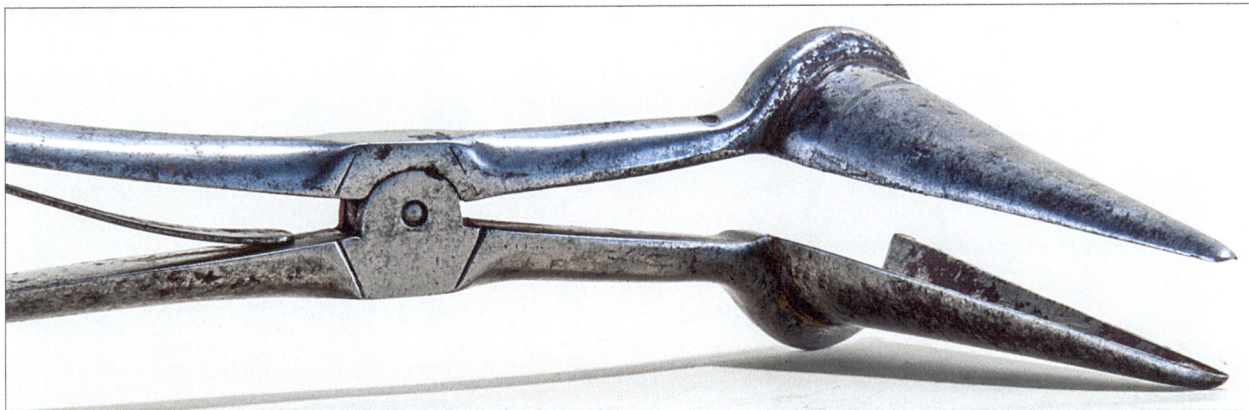

Bivalve aural speculum, Hildanus style.

dismissed them as "Hildanus' instrument in a new, deteriorated form."[6]

The 19th century brought a tremendous explosion in both innovation and adaptation of ear specula. These efforts helped push otology to a new level of diagnostic and therapeutic capabilities that would ultimately help establish it as a medical specialty in its own right.

Modifications with regard to specula could be seen in the continued development of Hildanus' bivalve design. German otologist Robbi revised the design with scissor-like handles and screws to dilate and fix the two arms. He also made the lumen's cross-section elliptical and placed a thin, metal ridge around the tympanic pole.[7] Englishman John Harrison Curtis, who

Robi's bivalve speculum with scissor-like handles and a dilating screw (circa 1830).

opened England's second institution dedicated solely to patients with otological diseases in 1816, also modified the bivalve speculum in this way, according to Schmaltz. This Robbi-Curtis model was obviously used by Schmaltz as a template in designing his own speculum, which was much the same but did not include the metal ridge on the tympanic pole.[8]

Famed German otologist Wilhelm Kramer felt all the specula available at the time were inadequate and chose to create his own.[9] Kramer's design was of the Hildanus school and reverted to a simpler construction than the Robbi-Curtis apparatus. A tapering, cylindrical, bivalve funnel was situated atop handles and a spring mechanism positioned between the handles. While Kramer's speculum was not the first of its kind — nor did it differ entirely from what was already available — he is credited with popularizing the use of a bivalve speculum. This attribution was made possible by his own fame and far-reaching influence within the field. Kramer's lasting impact can be seen in that his speculum design continued to bear his name and was available in major medical supply catalogues well into the 1900s.

Kramer was a fierce advocate of a symptom-based approach to maladies of the ear. This philosophy would dominate otology for most of the first half of the 19th century, but it eventually succumbed to a pathophysiological approach to disease. "[Kramer] adamantly opposed pathologic anatomy … and his system based on symptomatology was doomed to collapse with the advancement of modern otology," writes Politzer.[10] Kramer's style of teaching and professional interaction is outlined by Prosper Ménière in the introduction to his translation of Kramer's *Disease of the Ear*:

"Mr. Kramer prides himself on being frank; he goes straight to the point. His criticism is quick; these behaviors, which have their source as an attempt at a high degree of honesty, give his style a quality rooted in rough and hostile forms which are hard to tolerate in our language. I believe it is proper to soften their sharpness a little, and I took it upon myself to cut off some useless roughness. Science, once a little smoother, does not lose its merit. One can instruct without punishing the ignorant, and a little kindness does no harm."[11]

Despite evidence of fundamental differences between Ménière and Kramer, and between French and German cultures, both men played major roles in the development of otology.

A year after Kramer described his speculum in 1836, fellow German Karl Gustave Lincke published specula of his own design in the first of three volumes of his *Handbuch der Theoret und Praktischen Ohrenheilkunde*.[12] Fundamentally consistent with Kramer's — a bivalve, circular funnel on two handles — Lincke's design

Kramer's bivalve aural specula. The speculum in the middle has a slight S-shape to the handle, consistent with the Linke design.

differed in two primary ways: His speculum lacked a spring mechanism, and its handles bent in an S-shape away from their point of contact with the outer opening of the funnel, rather than dropping down at right angles.[13]

For the sake of completeness, two more bivalve specula designed by Charriere and Spangenberg were very much like the Hildanus design.

French surgeon Jean-Pierre Bonnafont and Friedrich Hofmann of Germany, a small-town general practitioner, invented their own ear specula in 1834 and 1841, respectively. Their designs were meant to address the challenge of having to hold the handles of a bivalve

speculum in order to use it properly, which left the physician with only one hand available to maneuver other instrumentation. Thus, these specula were made to be self-holding, or *auto-statique*. Bonnafont's was a bivalve speculum that used a screw and an externally placed stirrup mechanism to open the two arms and keep them in that position. This device was presumably used with an illuminating device similar to his otoscope. Similarly designed specula by other inventors were also used in fields such as endoscopy and gynecology.[14,15] Hofmann presented his self-holding speculum. From the descriptions, this speculum was a complex design, involving "a metallic double funnel consisting of an upper and a lower funnel part. The former portion ran into three arms which, by immediate action of a screw device, belonging to the lower funnel part, could be made to open or close at will."[16]

The true self-holding abilities of these specula — especially Bonnafont's — were somewhat in doubt. Key-Aberg felt their value was limited to a "dilatorium in the case of a certain degree of swelling of the external walls of the auricular tube. The instrument must always be held fast by the observer's hand."[17]

As previously noted, the bivalve speculum was widely popular among the top otologists of the 19th century, including Kramer and J.M. Gaspard Itard. During the same period, however, some otologists advocated the use of a speculum that more closely resembled the modern design. In 1823 Nicolas Deleau of France described his own specula auris, an undivided metal tube without a shaft. In 1827, Neuburg designed a long, horn-shaped speculum that was also one piece and lacked a shaft.[18] Thus it would seem Deleau was the first to invent this type of speculum, although Politzer attributes this contribution to Neuburg. Still other authors credit Ignaz Gruber of Vienna with inventing the first one-piece funnel speculum in 1838.[19] Gruber's speculum had a removable shaft and was conical in shape. He was said to have used it primarily for protecting the skin around the ear during the application

Neuberg or Deleau speculum, made from gold and platinum.

of potentially noxious fluid within the ear canal.[20] Nonetheless, undivided speculum designs by Deleau and Neuburg went largely unnoticed due to the popularity of the bivalve design at that time. This would soon change, as demonstrated

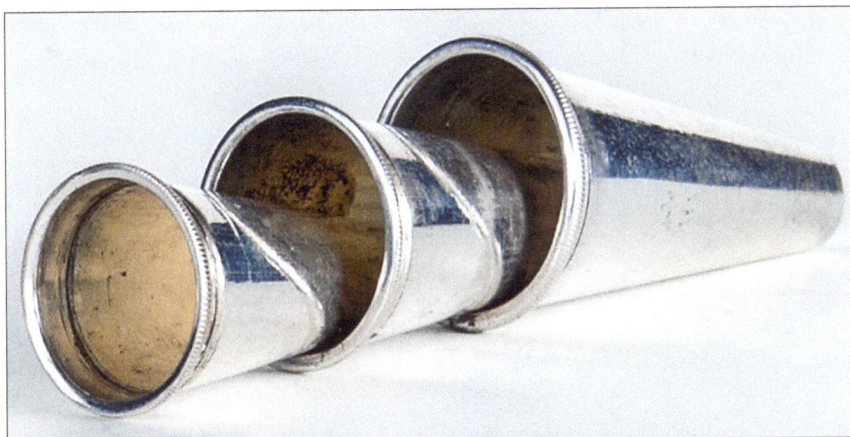

Set of Wilde specula.

by Politzer's opinion: "The older bivalve speculum has justly become obsolete on account of its deficiencies."[21]

It would not be until 1844, when Wilde described his preferred speculum design in *The Dublin Journal of Medical Science*, that the unbroken tubular speculum would gain popularity among English physicians. On a visit to Vienna, Wilde observed Gruber using his speculum with light from Kramer's lamp. Thus, it is Gruber to whom Wilde gives credit for inspiring his own design. Wilde's speculum was conical in shape like Gruber's, but its outer opening was slightly larger. Wilde wrote that he had tried varying shapes and sizes — and even painted the speculum's inner aspect a matte black — but found the design he published and continued to use to be the best. He concluded that "all the instruments heretofore invented for examining or operating upon the external auditory passages were defective, as a means of transmitting light, which is the only real object of a speculum."[22] Elsewhere, Wilde spoke to his dislike for bivalve specula due to their difficulty in handling and the lack of need for a speculum with such a capacity to dilate the ear canal:

"To attempt any degree of dilation of the auditory passage by means of instruments shows a want of anatomical knowledge in their inventors, as the most any speculum can effect is to straighten the external cartilaginous portion of the tube."[23]

At the midpoint of the 19th century, Englishman Joseph Toynbee published new design for ear speculum in the *Lancet*. Toynbee's design incorporated an oval lumen to better fit the shape of the ear canal. This was an aspect of the circular specula he found particularly undesirable:

"It will be immediately apparent that when a circular tube is introduced into this oval-shaped meatus, it may press against its anterior and

Set of Schmaltz-Erhard specula, manufactured by Sklar (USA).

posterior walls, while a considerable space above or below remains unoccupied by it. As a rule, it is impossible by means of an instrument thus shaped to obtain a view of more than a small portion of the meatus or of the membrana tympani at a time; and in cases where the meatus is very small, the circular tube does not give passage to a sufficient quantity of luminous rays to enable the surface of the membrana tympani to be discerned."[24]

Many regard Toynbee as the father of British otology, and his career parallels a greater changing of the guard in the field. Early in the second half of the 19th century, otologists were shifting away from the symptomatology made popular by Kramer in favor of the philosophy of pathological anatomy. This transition was made possible by advancements across many fields, including histology and physiology, and their application to the understanding of disease processes. With this more detailed scientific knowledge, medical practice began to segment into various specialties. Toynbee's career exemplifies this transition. After advanced training as assistant curator to the Royal College of Surgeons and Fellow of the Royal Society, he was rewarded with an appointment as aural surgeon at Saint Mary's Hospital. This was the first general hospital to give distinction to cases of otological disease, a sign of the emergence of otology as its own specialty. When Toynbee published *Diseases of the Ear* in 1860, it was regarded as one of the most complete and insightful texts in the field.

Seemingly every leading European otologist of the 19th century worked diligently to

Politzer or Boucheron specula, manufactured by Allen & Hanburry's Ltd., London.

develop his own method of examining the ear. This drive to create the most practical techniques and instruments is responsible for the surge of specula designs that emerged in the mid- to late 1800s. Schmaltz invented a funnel-shaped speculum in 1846, and Julius Erhard published a speculum design in an 1859 publication, *Rationell Otiatrik*. Erhard's was funnel-shaped like Toynbee's but had a circular lumen like the Gruber-Wilde specula.[25] In 1862, Politzer presented a similarly designed speculum: funnel-shaped with a circular section. Politzer altered his own design further in 1878 by making it out of hard, black rubber rather than the reflective metal that was the status quo.[26] Politzer style specula have also been made of glass. An example of which is in the Touma Collection.

Interestingly, though, Politzer felt the design of an ear speculum had little bearing on the success of an examination. When discussing the available solid specula, he said, "Their dissimilarity as well as their shape is of little importance in the examination of the ear."[27]

Politzer's contributions to the tools of otoscopy are limited to his speculum design. His overall contribution to the field of otology, however, is difficult to overstate. Many consider him one of the most eminent otologists of all time — if not the most eminent. He studied medicine in one of otology's capitals, Vienna, under Josef Hyrtl; became more focused in auditory physiology under Ménière in Paris; and learned modern aural surgical techniques under the guidance of Toynbee in London. His original contributions include an atlas of otoscopy; textbooks on diseases of the ear, anatomy, and histology; and a book on the history of otology. He invented several diagnostic and therapeutic aids, including the

Set of Hartmann-style specula.

speculum mentioned above, an acoumeter, and an eponymous method of permeating the Eustachian tube. Emblematic of the changing tide in the mid-19th century, Politzer was an anatomic pathologist and was the first to describe many pathologic conditions such as otosclerosis, labyrinthitis, and atelectasis of the ear.[28]

German otologist Anton von Tröltsch was not fond of Politzer's vulcanite material and used silver to make a speculum of the same dimensions.[29] While von Tröltsch and Politzer were more significant in their day, inventor Arthur Hartmann created a speculum in 1881 that would see just as much if not more future use than either of their models. "From all appearances, it is a variety of the von Tröltsch-Politzer type of ear speculum that bears Hartmann's name in the catalogues of the instrument makers," Key-Aberg writes.[30] The simple, bell-shaped design of the Hartmann

speculum should be familiar to many modern physicians, as it is one of the more popular designs still in use today.[31] Among many other devices, Hartmann also invented the first audiometer.[32]

Around the same time Politzer introduced his speculum, German otologist Johann Lucae proposed that the tympanic pole of the ear speculum be cut obliquely. According to Key-Aberg, this was an interesting idea and, "possibly in some slight degree, was an aid to the inspection of the auricular tube, but hardly the real aim of otoscopy."[33]

The next breakthrough in speculum design came in 1870 when Clarence Blake made known his design for an operating speculum. Based out of Harvard and the Massachusetts Eye and Ear Infirmary, Blake employed the help of Boston physicist and inventor Edward S. Ritchie in constructing an operating otoscope.[34,35]

"It consists of a hard rubber (Poltizer's)

speculum of the largest size, fitted with a metallic rim, to which is attached a revolving prism and an arm, bearing its outer end a lens of about an inch focus; this arm is movable[.] … It is not claimed for this instrument that it at all supersedes the head mirror of Von Tröltsch, but it is certainly of great advantage in the more complicated operations."[36]

Frederic Edward Rudolph Voltolini, an otologist from Breslau, also designed an operating speculum. According to his colleague Josef Gruber, "for the performance of operations, Voltolini recommends the use of a speculum with a lateral opening."[37] Voltolini was certainly one of Europe's leading minds in the field during the mid- to late 19th century. He and Bonnafont were the first to use a tube in an attempt to keep a myringotomy site patent.[38]

Near the turn of the 20th century, a French otologist by the name of Boucheron invented a speculum known for its utility both in inspecting the tympanic membrane and as a surgical tool, which is fitting as he was involved in early efforts at stapes mobilizations.[39] The speculum is funnel-shaped and circular in section and appears to be a cross between the Hartmann and Politzer designs. Boucheron's speculum was a popular design that still carries his name and remains available from a variety of surgical supply companies. A few years later, in 1903, Gustav Brühl described a demonstration speculum: "an ordinary ear funnel in whose inner opening there [was] arranged a little metal pin which, in the act of examining the ear, points out that part of the membrana tympani that is to be demonstrated."[40]

While several more speculum designs emerged that are not discussed here, these examples give plentiful evidence of early otologists' dedication to advancing their field. Additionally, as with other devices in otoscopy around the mid-19th century, each practitioner had his own opinions and preferences regarding examining patients. These differences in opinion are perhaps magnified with specula as compared to otoscopes; specula are simpler in design, making them relatively easy and inexpensive to produce. One good example was patented in 1889 by James Maloney. He suggested making a speculum out of firm paper coated with protective wax and proposed that its cost would be so small that it could be thrown away after a single use.[41]

Other interesting designs are included in this chapter. The hybrid self-retaining bivalve speculum has a handle that is much smaller than other bivalve designs, and its main function was to help spread the valves apart. In the early 20th century, an attempt was made to convert to using the bivalve speculum with a spring popularized by Kramer. As modern practitioners will know, the design did not

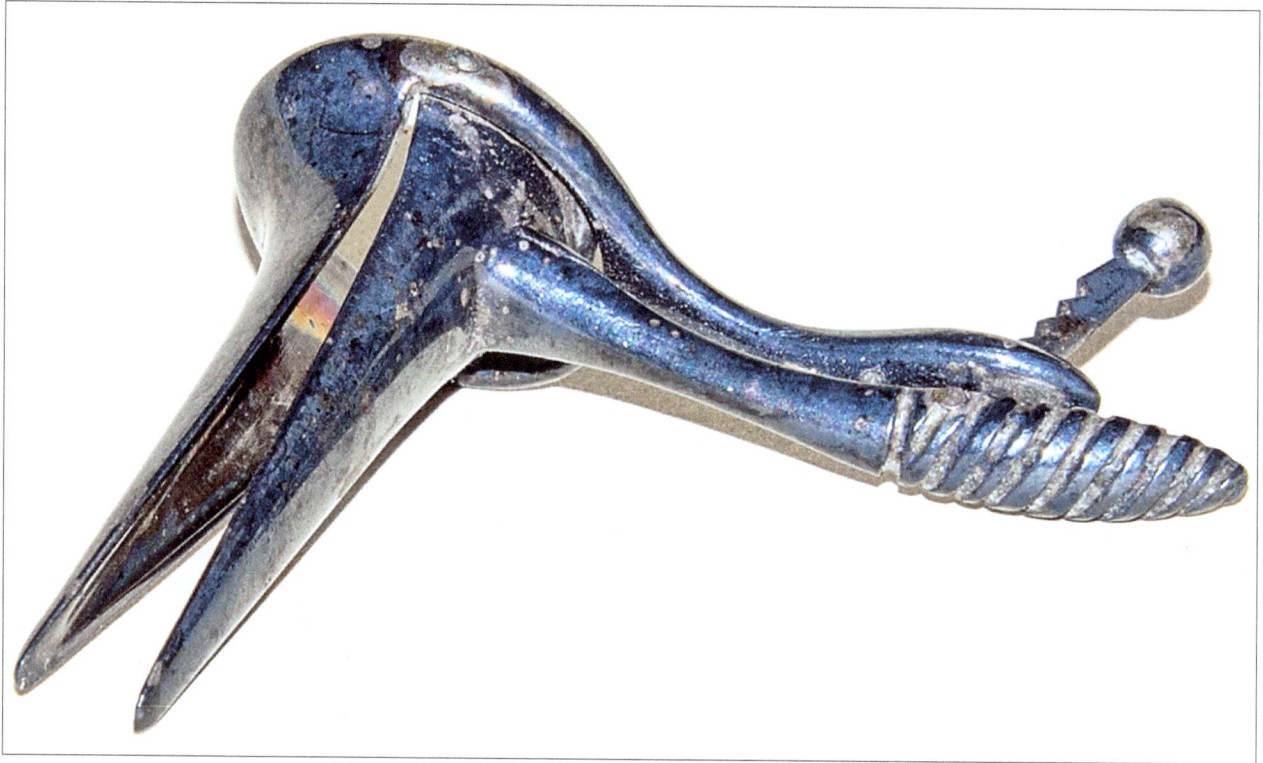

Bonnafont or Spier's self-retaining aural speculum with locking mechanism.

regain widespread use. The Touma collection has a unique Hartmann speculum with a shield and a handle; the reason behind this design is unknown. The "Earscope," designed by an unknown inventor, was presumably used to gauge the size of the meatus in order to choose the appropriate speculum.

Glass funnel-type speculum similar to Politzer's early design (1860s).

Bivalve aural speculum with spring steel handle.

Handheld Hartmann or Politzer ear speculum with circular shield.

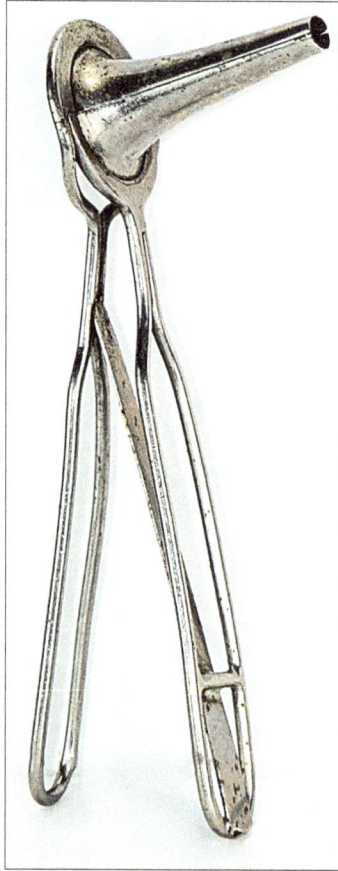

Early 20th-century handheld bivalve ear speculum with spring.

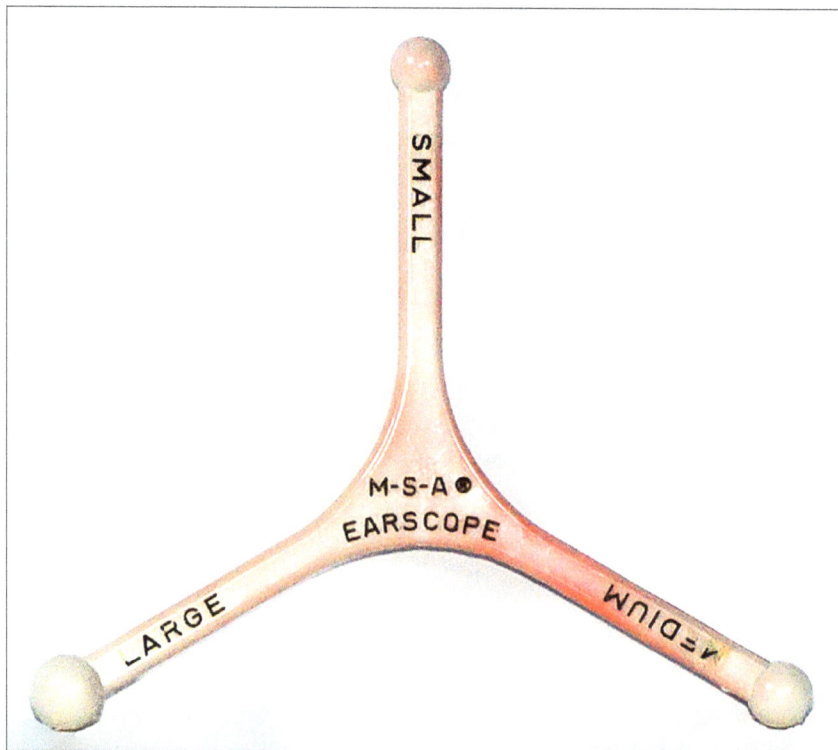

"Earscope" meatus gauge (1930s).

ILLUMINATION

Adequate lighting of the ear canal and eardrum are essential to making proper diagnoses and initiating treatment. Before the 17th century, however, physicians relied on ambient light to illuminate the ear canal, leaving them at the mercy of the weather and the angle of the sun. Alcohol and oil lamps were used when sunlight was not available. Furthermore, gaining sufficient illuminating power without some means of concentrating light into the small, angled canal made investigations difficult. In the early 1600s, these problems were addressed successfully by Girolamo Fabrizio of Italy. He used the refractive power of a water-filled flask to concentrate light from a wax candle into a beam capable of illuminating the ear canal. This allowed him to more accurately ascertain the whereabouts of foreign bodies, which he could then carefully remove with tweezers or hooked instruments.[42] Fabrizio, also known as Fabricius ab Aquapendente, studied with Gabriele Falloppio at the University of Padua, where Falloppio taught anatomy and botany

Brass alcohol lamp, made in the United States.

and practiced surgery. Esteemed among the greatest anatomists of their time, both men made multiple discoveries and original characterizations of structures in the human body, such as the course of the facial nerve within the temporal bone in the facial canal that carries Falloppio's name.[43]

More than a century passed before another inventor, British military surgeon Archibald Cleland, would improve upon Fabrizio's idea. Cleland positioned a biconvex lens in line with a wax candle by means of an adjustable holder and harnessed its refraction to concentrate the light into the ear. Like Fabrizio, Cleland used this illuminating power to gain accurate information about the presence and location of foreign bodies within the ear canal, allowing more precision in attempting their removal. He presented this device, along with instruments used for catheterization of the Eustachian tube, in *Philosophical Transactions* in 1739.[44] His illumination device was celebrated for decades by many, including von Tröltsch and Wilde. But the exposed light of the candle proved a limitation, because, as noted by Johann Peter Frank, "the observing eye was, without exception, dazzled by the naked light."[45]

This lamp uses the concentrating power of its concave reflector, with double wicks, similar to Bozzini's 1807 invention.

In 1807 Philipp Bozzini of Germany, considered the inventor of the first endoscope, improved upon Cleland's design by substituting a concave mirror for the convex lens. This design successfully allowed the observer to look into the ear canal without the dazzling effect that had proven so troublesome. Bozzini did not experience much success with his device, however, as it failed to generate favorable illumination power.[46] The greater triumph for Bozzini, and otoscopy as a whole, was this first use of a concave mirror to concentrate and redirect a light source — a concept otolaryngologists have embraced long since.

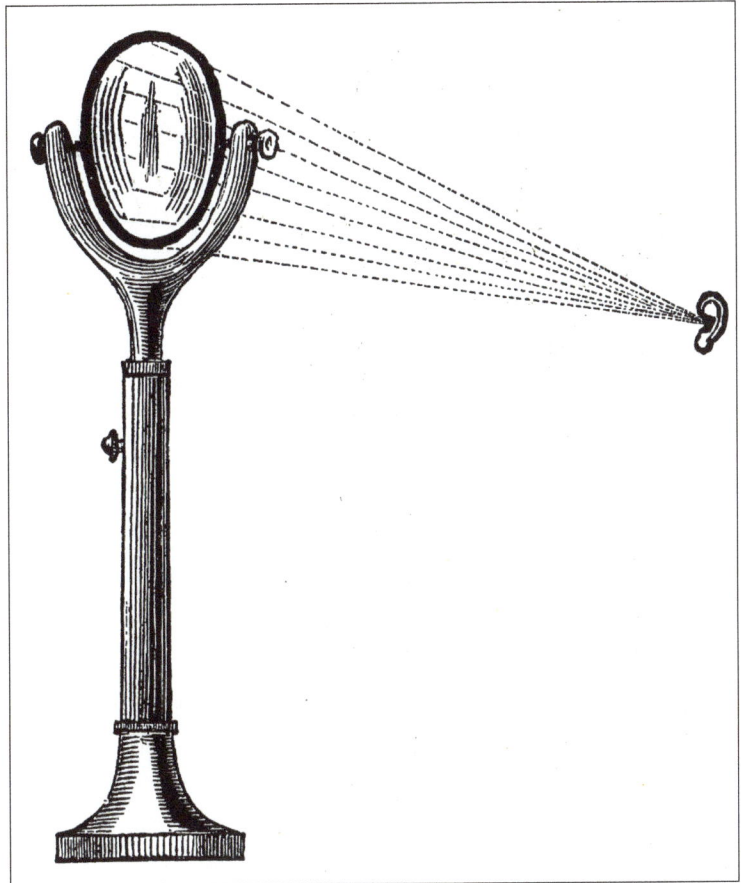

(Left) Bockett microscope lamp by Collins of London. This lamp relies on its biconvex lens to concentrate the light on the flame. This principle was employed in otology originally by Nicholas Deleau in 1823. (Right) His illumination device employed a bi-convex lens to concentrate a light source (1823).

In 1823, Deleau presented two devices for casting light into the ear canal in a piece entitled *Description d'un instrument etc.*[47] One creation, more consistent with designs of years past, used a biconvex lens on a stand to concentrate sunlight, much as Cleland had already done. The second, a more novel device, involved two concave metal mirrors facing each other on a metal stand with a centrally positioned wax candle. The medial mirror had a central perforation for the passage of rays of light concentrated by the lateral mirror. This was the first use of a centrally perforated mirror; however, it would not be until two decades later that a mirror of this type would be used in its more familiar capacity. While his contributions to viewing the external ear canal were limited, Deleau enjoyed a celebrated career as one of France's leading otologists. Eventually becoming head of the Department of Ear Disease at the Hospice des Orphelins in Paris, Deleau deserves mention among the giants of his country, like Itard and Ménière.[48]

Two years later, in 1825, Thomas Buchanan introduced his own illumination device in *Illustrations of Acoustic Surgery*. The *inspector auris*, as Buchanan called it, used a tube directed at the ear. Two biconvex lenses were placed in the tube, and a ballooning lateral portion housed a wax candle that sat between a concave mirror and the more lateral of the two biconvex lenses within the tube. The design was not fundamentally different from Bozzini's but was "one of a more complicated nature," in Key-Aberg's opinion.[49] Fascinated by the external ear and its effect on the physiology of hearing, the true nature of which proved elusive to him, Buchanan took the meticulous external ear canal measurements cited earlier. On a more practical note, he may have also been the first otologist to advocate pulling the pinna posteriorly and superiorly to gain an improved view of the tympanic membrane.[50]

Kramer presented his own illumination system, known as an ear lamp, in 1836. This did not necessarily improve upon Buchanan's design, but it does deserve mention for using

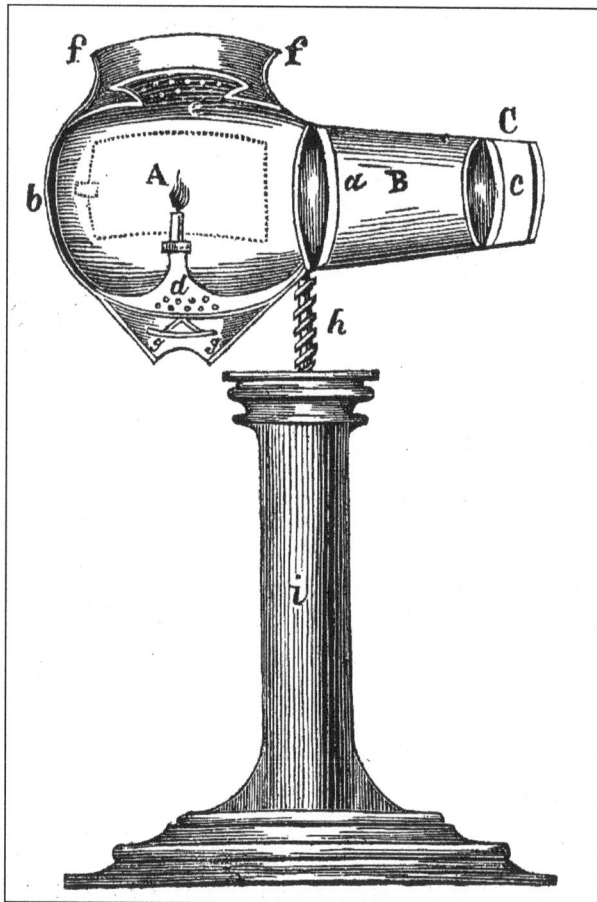

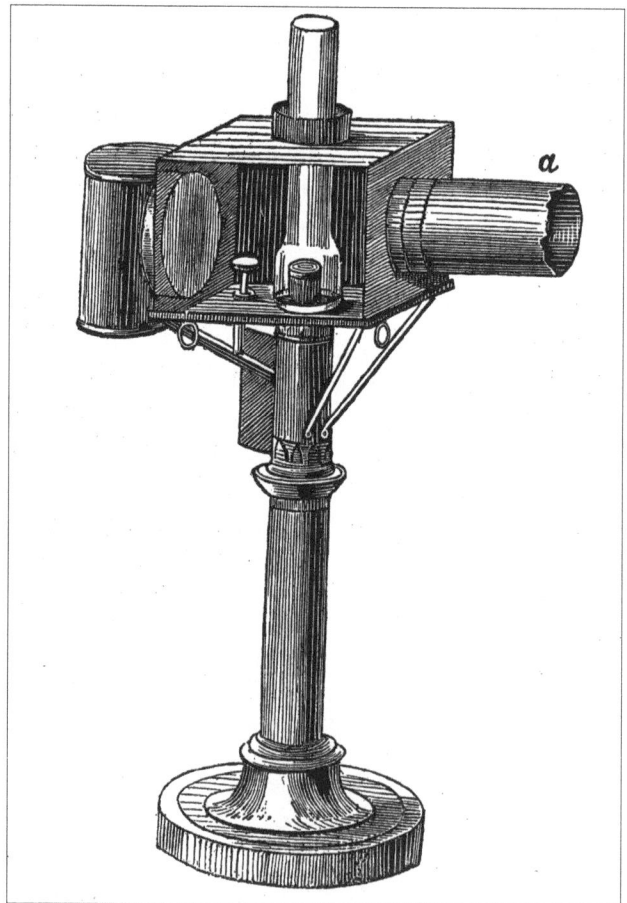

(Left) Thomas Buchanan's Inspector Auris—1825. (Right) Kramer's ear lamp —1836, was similar to Buchanan's Inspector Auris, but used an Argand lamp as opposed to a wax candle.

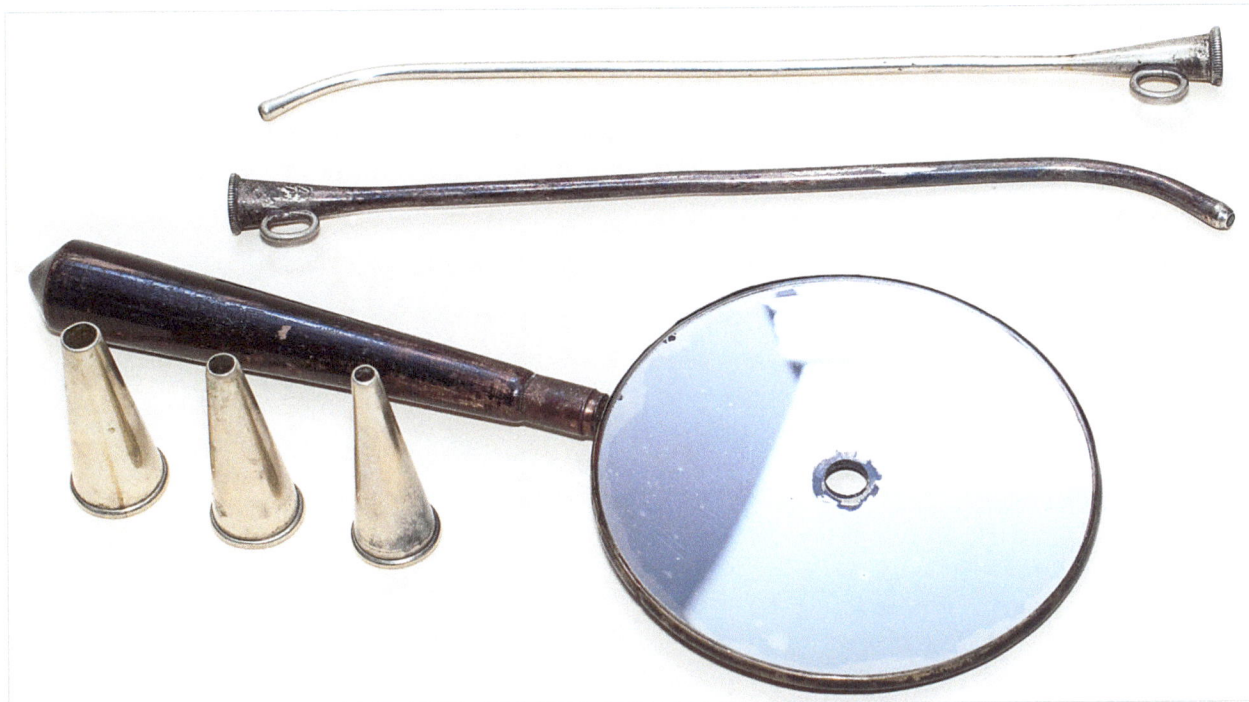

Set of a mirror, Wilde-style specula and Eustachian tube catheters, likley dating to the mid- to late-19th century.

an oil lamp rather than a candle as its light source, which, according to Wilde, enhanced its illuminating power.[51] The only other notable difference between the Kramer and Buchanan devices was that the former used only one bi-convex lens. Although Kramer's device allowed him to inspect patients' ears day or night, he maintained that "sunlight remains the only satisfactory illumination medium as far as it depends on carefully examining important pathological changes of the hearing channel and namely the tympanic membrane."[52] Many contemporaries, including Wilde, would agree, saying the light required for the most delicate procedures was obtainable only from the natural source of the sun.[53]

As mentioned above, the first use of a centrally perforated concave mirror was seen in 1823 with Deleau's device. However, it was not until 1841 that it would be used in the manner familiar to modern-day otolaryngologists. In the January edition of a small publication, *Caspers Wochenschrift fur die gesammte Heilkunde*, Friedrich Hofmann made known his use of a centrally perforated concave mirror to illuminate the ear canal:

"By means of a concave mirror perforated in the centre, the sun-light is thrown into the auricular tube which, when one looks through the hole in the mirror, can be seen illuminated. If the sun is obscured by clouds, it is often possible to obtain a satisfactory illumination

Set of a mirror and Erhard-style specula contained in a leather case. The plaque reads:
"University of New York Session of 1872-73 Prize for the best Examination of Diseases of the Ear to
Charles E. Hall, M.D. From Professor C.B. St. John Roosa, M.D."

by means of reflected daylight. If this be not enough, however, artificial light must be resorted to, either in the form of two wax-candles placed close to the aperture in the mirror, or else, and decidedly preferably, of an Argand burner. These artificial lights must be used in a dark room."[54]

In the same publication, Hofmann presented his *autostatique* ear speculum and reported on the case of a deaf patient from whose tympanic membrane he removed small substances by using a Daniel's spoon and his illuminating device. According to the report, the patient's hearing returned to normal after the procedure.[55] Hofmann's ingenuity was eventually mentioned by contemporaries. Frank and Rau, Hofmann's brother-in-law, made note of it in 1845 and 1856, respectively; but this great idea did not initially take hold. Perhaps because Hofmann practiced in the small town of Bergsteinfurt, far from a major urban center, and published his idea where it experienced little circulation, it would take the involvement of someone more directly connected to the epicenters of otology for the

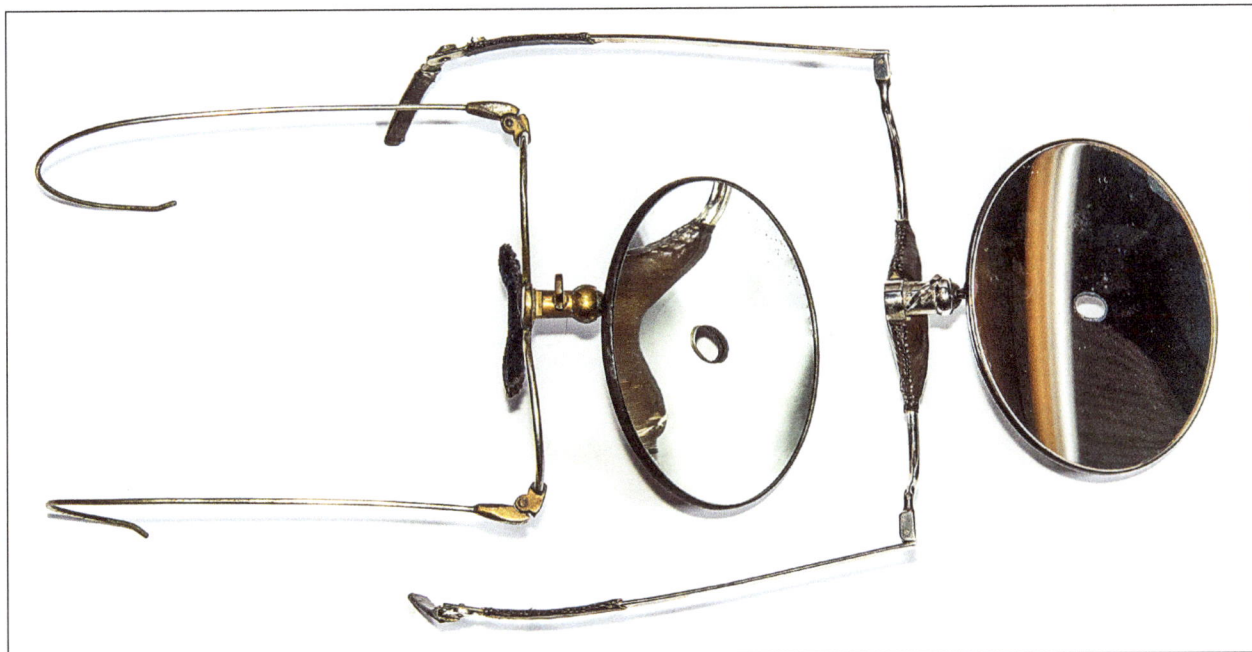

Eyeglasses-style head mirrors as proposed by Anton von Tröltsch.

centrally perforated mirror to attract attention.[56]

In 1855 Anton von Tröltsch demonstrated his use of a perforated concave mirror to the Society of German Doctors in Paris.[57] With his backing — but no acknowledgment of Hofmann's original achievement — this method began to gain popularity. It is difficult to discern whether von Tröltsch was aware of Hofmann's prior success with the mirror, but the fact that Frank mentioned the Hofmann mirror in a widely used 1845 textbook suggests the possibility that von Tröltsch was familiar with the general practitioner's ingenuity. In fact, he conceded in an 1868 publication that Hofmann had been the first to present the use of the perforated mirror. Though this admission appeared in smaller font, it solidified Hofmann's ownership of the advancement to at least some degree.[58]

While not technically the first to suggest it, von Tröltsch deserves mention for popularizing this use of a mirror. Authors into the next century describe the use of a head mirror and credit him for its invention, supporting the notion that he was the one to give the idea broad exposure. Von Tröltsch also advocated using a headband to secure the mirror in position and free the physician's hands.[59] Key-Aberg writes, "von Tröltsch himself proposed that the perforated concave mirror should be arranged on the rim of a pair of spectacles, and, by degree, others adopted it to holding devices of other kinds."[60]

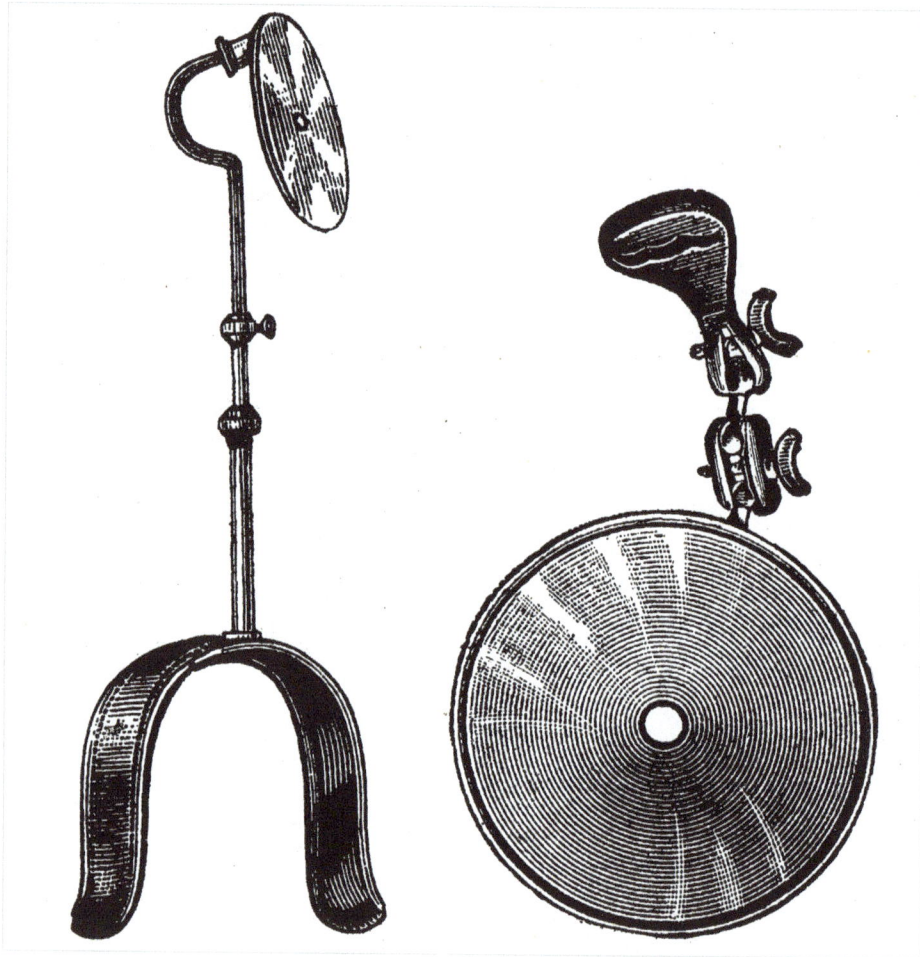

(Left) A shoulder stand and (Right) a mirror held between the physician's teeth exemplify the means employed to allow hands-free use of reflective mirrors.

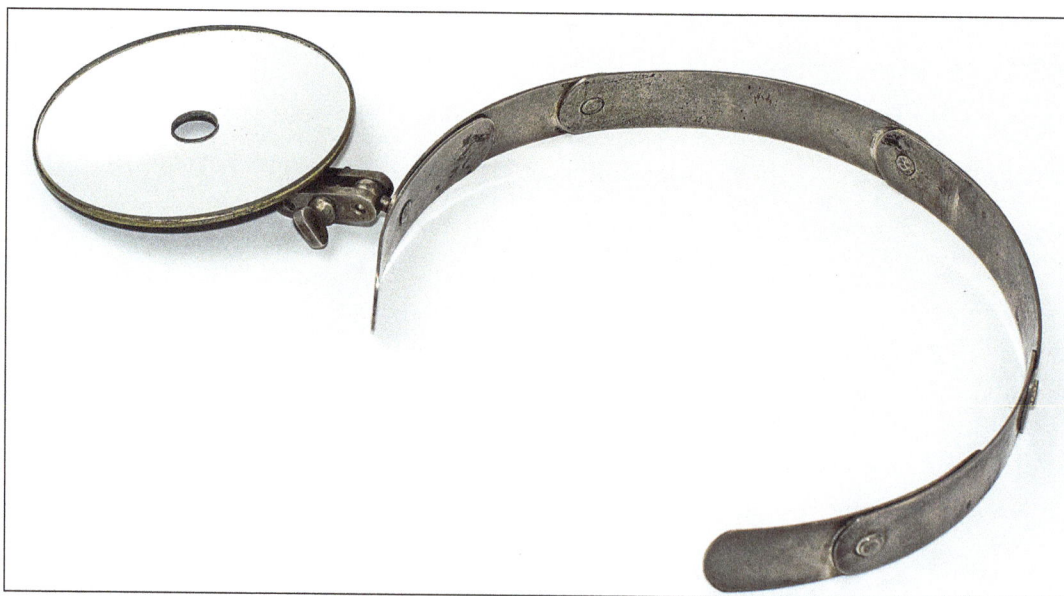

Worrall collapsible spring headband head mirror.

The number of ways otologists devised to hold the mirror in place seems to have rivaled their wide variety of ear specula designs. One approach involved a forehead band of elastic material with an attached joint to which the mirror could be secured and adjusted to redirect the light as needed. Other examples include an apparatus with the mirror positioned on a stand that extended from a base made to straddle the physician's shoulder, a mouthpiece, and metal bridges that ran either over the crown of the head or circumferentially.[61] Another interesting design was Worrall's folding spring headband, made of folded metal segments that were secured over the crown of the head but could be collapsed for easier storage.[62]

After the advent of the head mirror, originality in the realm of illumination techniques was in short supply. In 1842, Polansky advocated the use of a silver spoon to redirect and concentrate the light of a candle, which Ménière had actually done a year before.[63] John Avery, a surgeon at Charing Cross Hospital in London, mounted in 1844 a centrally perforated concave mirror and a candle on a piece of headgear, a seemingly precarious construction. Avery's device was meant to be used as a laryngoscope to assist in viewing the vocal folds in the larynx; but

with modifications, he was able to examine the ear as well.[64] Others, including Wilde, also used this technique for illumination.[65] Warren, also from London, used a prism to concentrate a beam of light onto the tympanic membrane. Von Grauvogel would eventually perfect this process in 1848 with a convex lens. In 1849, Schmaltz invented the *tubus a la laterna magica*, which used mirrors and lenses to throw light

A silver spoon could be used in a manner similar to a concave mirror as advocated by Polansky.

into the ear, harkening back to the Buchanan and Kramer designs.

Devices like Schmaltz's and the ear lamps made by Buchanan and Kramer were used mostly to shine a beam of light directly into the ear canal. Toynbee mentioned devices that offered additional means to the same end, including the gas-powered Segalas lamp and the Miller lamp, which used a wax candle. He described these, both of which used circular

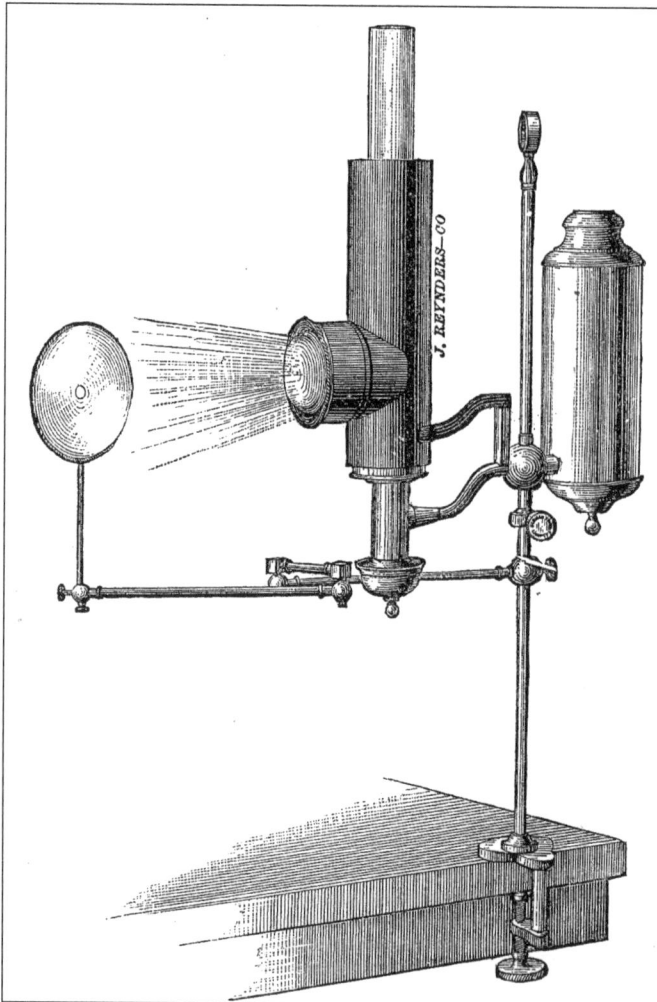

Mackenzie condenser. Illumination came from gas, alcohol lamps, or electric bulbs.

reflectors to redirect light and could be operated with one hand, as simple and economical illumination options.[67] However, with the invention of the head mirror, many otologists opted to use an indirect source of light. In *A Manual of Otology*, Gorham Bacon writes, "When good natural light cannot be obtained, artificial light should be substituted, such as that from an Argand burner, with or without a Mackenzie's bull's-eye lens[.] ... An excellent light is that obtained from a candle fitted in a holder and supplied with a lens."[68]

These lamps could be placed on a table or mounted on a wall and had adjustable joints to facilitate repositioning.[69] Other constructions also incorporated adjustability to suit the physician's lighting requirements. Stands made from metal poles secured to a table by a vice, for example, could be modified by adding and subtracting various parts and moving the stand or its appendages in space. In 1883, Oren Pomeroy, a surgeon at the Manhattan Eye and Ear Hospital, provided an illustration of a stand to which was attached a lamp with a Mackenzie condenser and centrally perforated reflecting mirror.[70] A construction like this freed both hands and was essentially a larger-scale version of early otoscopes.

The expanding availability of electricity

and Edison's invention of the incandescent light bulb in 1879 provided otologists with another optional light source. This novel source of illumination would be used in a number of ways, some familiar and others more innovative. As with gas lamps and wax candles, an electric lamp could be set on a table or mounted to a wall to provide ambient light. Many also opted to continue the previous use of wall brackets that permitted movement and adjustment.[71] Edward Dench, professor of diseases of the ear at the University of Bellevue Hospital Medical College, built his own stand, which allowed candles, gas lamps, or electric lamps to be positioned as he saw fit.[72] In this fashion, electricity provided another dependable light source for physicians who required indirect illumination of the ear canal. While the source was new, the concept and related instrument were not. The head mirror continued to be the preferred way to redirect light into the auditory meatus. Further development of the electric light source lead to the introduction of condensing lens situated in front of the light bulb such as the Bockel light source, patented in 1880, and continued to be used for almost a century.

The electric headlamp would be this new age's novel approach to illuminating the ear

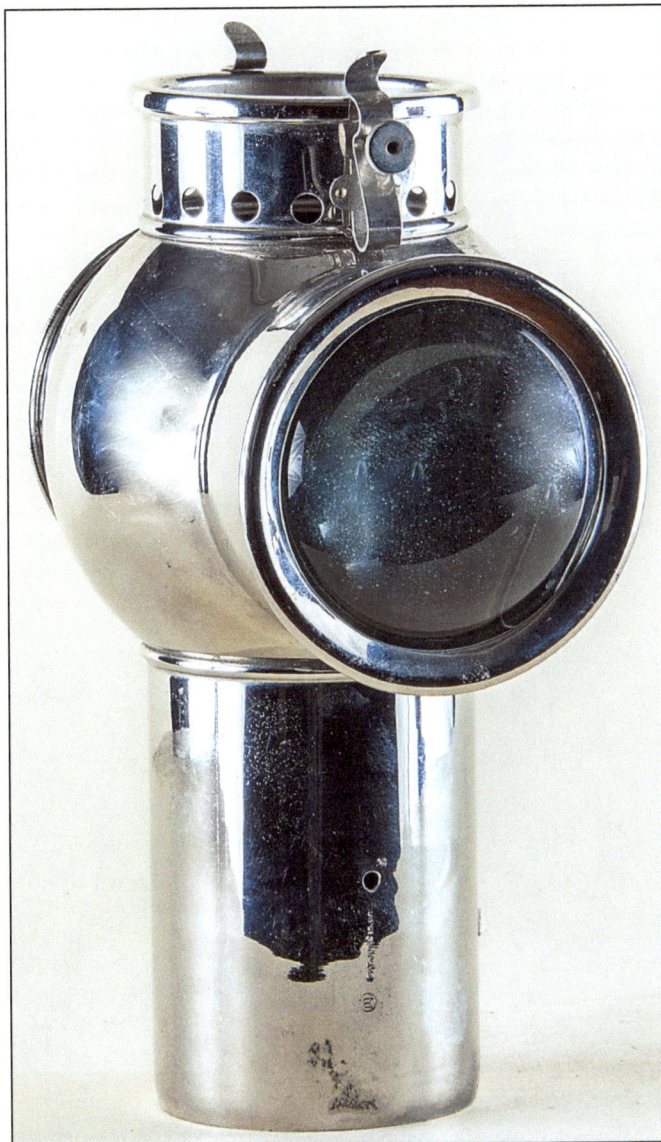

Early electric Boekel light source with condensing lens, patented in 1880 by Philadelphia-based inventors William and Julius Boekel. This design continued to be used into the 1970s.

canal. Interestingly, the headlamp would undergo an evolution similar to that of its non-electric precursors. The simplest initial form consisted of an electric lamp positioned on the forehead with the light shining directly toward the object of interest. Charles Burnett provides an example of such a headlamp

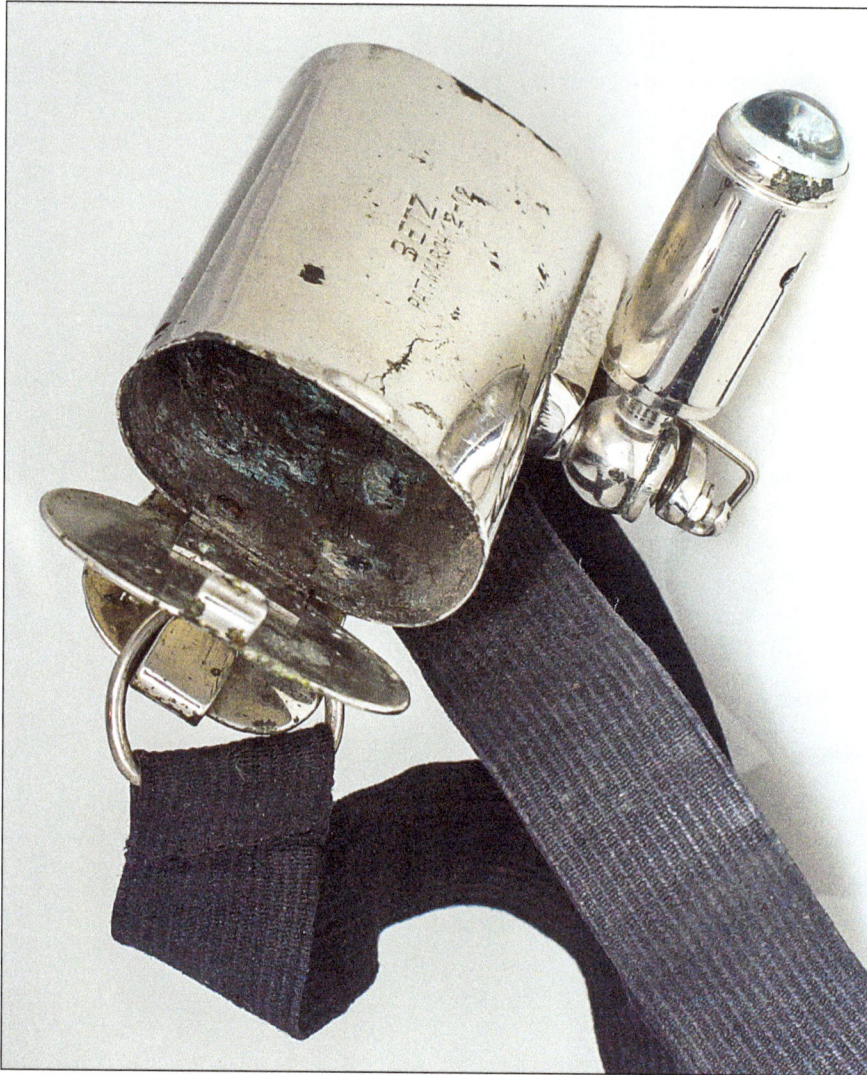

Battery-powered headlight manufatured and patented by Betz in 1912. It read: "Dr. Shumate, Reeds Spring, MD" with a five-cent postage stamp on the box.

an incandescent bulb in front of a reflecting surface that attaches to a coronal head strap by two ball-and-socket joints. The light connects to a transformer that allows for adjustable amounts of light, which in turn connects to a wall socket. Other headlights in the collection include a coronal type by Allen and Handburys, Ltd., sagittal headlight by Kayes Products, U.S., and Cameron headlight. They use bi-convex lens to concentrate the light. The collection has several battery-powered headlights including the Damon "contact model" which uses an elastic band to secure the incandescent bulb to the forehead, the Betz headlight with bi-convex lens, and a loop-type headlight. Battery power, of course, offered physicians the convenience of increased mobility and simplified operation during house calls. Philip Kerrison noted, however, that this convenience was not without its price: "The

in his 1901 textbook, along with a comment that should require no explanation: "Electric illumination by this means is the only form of artificial light that can safely be brought near the ear of the etherized patient."[73]

The Touma ENT Museum collection includes a number of these simple headlamps, two of which feature advances in power supplies. The Smith adjustable headlamp positions

Klaar's electric headlight with perforated concave mirror. It can be collapsed and stored in a relatively small can.

battery is supplied with six dry cells, which, unfortunately, must be renewed every four to five weeks. This, however, is a trifling disadvantage compared with the difficulties of inspection by other methods of illumination in private houses."[74]

The next advance in headlamps came from Alfred Kirstein, a pioneer in laryngoscopy and the first to perform direct examination of the interior of the larynx in 1895. He applied the concept of reflected light in his headlamp design.[75,76] An electric lamp positioned on the forehead was oriented toward a small, centrally perforated plane mirror, thereby reflecting a beam of light in line with the physician's sight. A shade, also perforated, was placed between the back of the mirror and the examiner's eye to protect from any glaring effect. Others expanded on this concept. Klaar's headlamp design, for example, employed a deep concave mirror with two perforations to concentrate the light of an electric bulb and allow binocular visualization and examination. Admittedly, the Kirstein and Klaar designs were technically indirect illuminating devices, but they still played significant roles in the

Kristein's "Good Lite" headlight with a perforated mirror to reflect and direct the light beam. The examiner can see through the perforation.

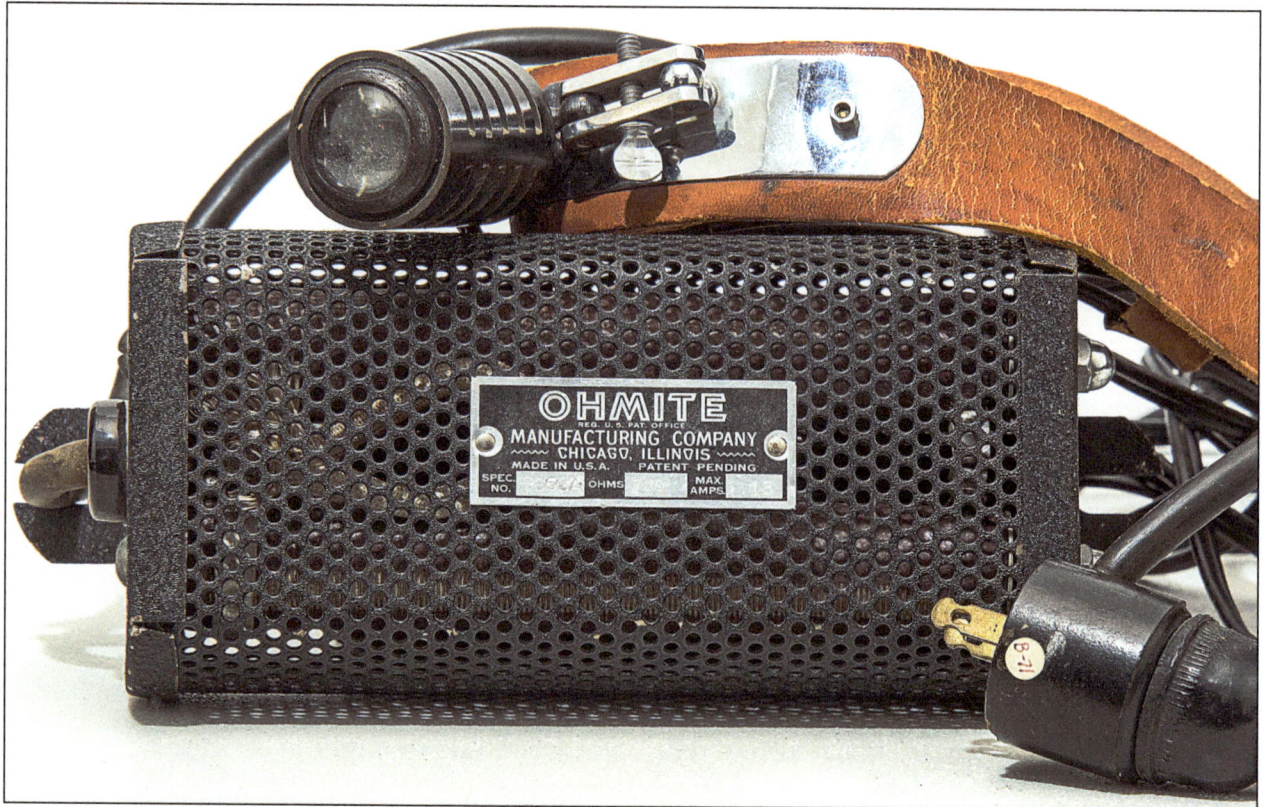

Early electric Hu-Friedy Headlight with an Ohmite power source.

evolution of the headlamp.

The next effort to concentrate light from an electric bulb on a headlamp involved placing the light in a housing behind a convex lens. The light was thereby concentrated and thrown forward from the illuminating apparatus. There are several headlamps of this type in the Touma collection. One, made by Hu-Friedy, uses an adjustable leather headband. Another, one of the more unusual applications of the concept, is the "Speclight," trademarked in 1925 by the Comprex Oscillator Corporation. The Speclight has a small incandescent bulb in a housing with an overlying biconvex lens that can be attached to a pair of eyeglasses with magnification power in the lower halves of the lenses. This device could be powered by a two-cell battery or via street electricity with a transformer that allowed for adjustability. A third example, known as the "Good Lite," combines the principles of the Kirstein design with a biconvex lens to concentrate the light.

Advances in electric lighting eventually led to the development of smaller lamps that could be suspended directly from a physician's forehead without obstructing visibility. One such device is shown in a 1927 text by New York surgeon Wendell Phillips.[77]

Growing use of optical fibers presented even more sophisticated illumination options for medical headlamps. Some advantages of fiber optics are outlined in the patent claim for a surgical headlight and light source developed by Frederick Wallace, assignor to American Cystoscope Makers:

"It is a further object of the present invention to provide an improved illumination device, particularly well-suited for carrying out medical examinations, surgical procedures, and the like, for directing a cool, high intensity light beam onto a work area[.] … It is another object of the present invention to provide an illumination apparatus, adapted to be worn on the head of the person, for directing a high intensity light beam at a viewing area in front of the eyes of the person, wherein the portion of the apparatus carried on the head is of significantly reduced size and weight compared to conventional head-mounted lamps heretofore known."[78]

As with the first use of electricity for a head-lamp, Wallace's 1966 invention demonstrates how quickly technological advances and constant improvements in diagnostic and operative devices can enhance the medical community's ability to provide higher levels of care.

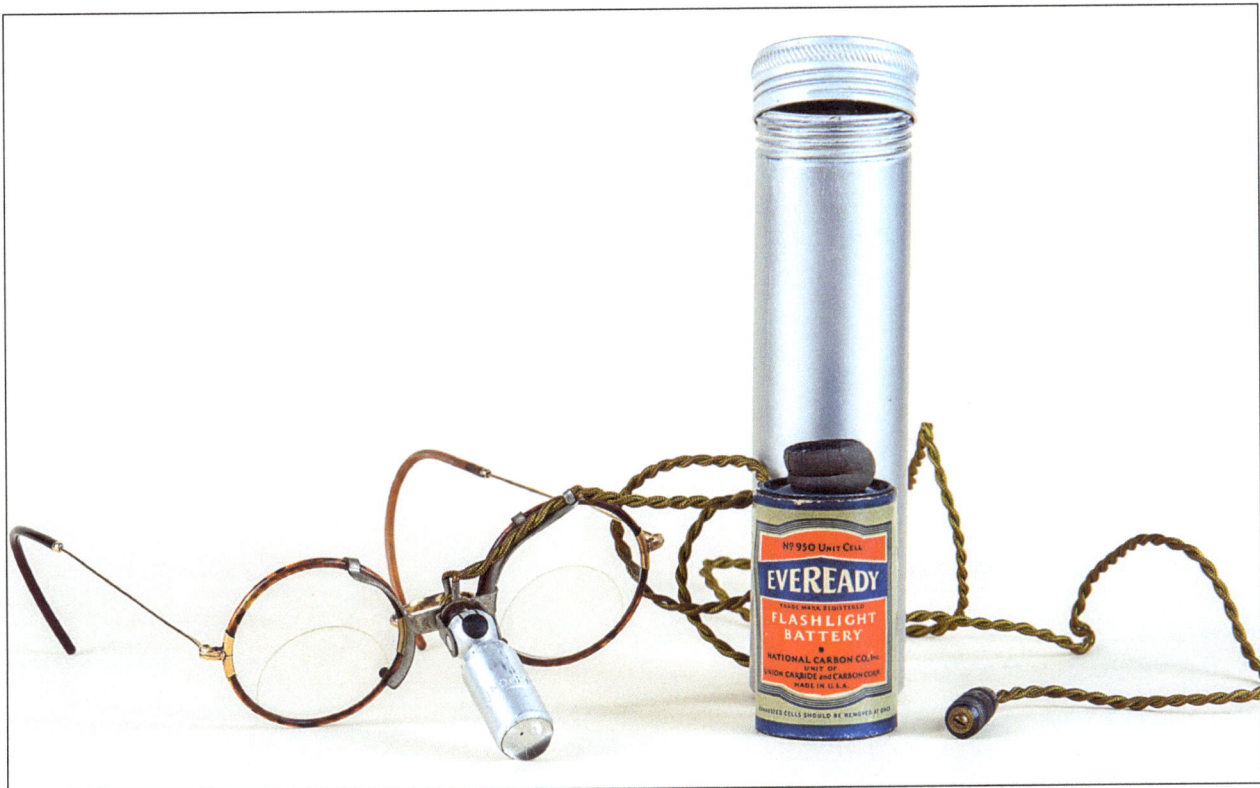

Battery-powered "speclight" mounted on eyeglasses.

Various glass alcohol lamps.

Components of a Collins' oil lamp.

Collins' oil lamp and condenser similar to
Kramer and Buchanan lamps. The light is
concentrated by a concave mirrored surface
and concentrating lens.

Battery-powered headlight and similar regular loupe

Jansen's coronal headlight by Allen and Hanburys Ltd. of London uses a bi-convex lens to concentrate its direct source of illumination.

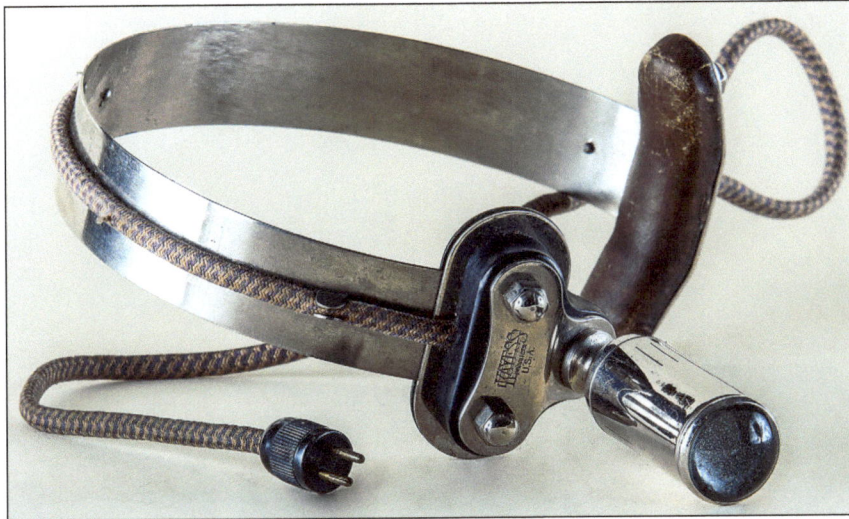

Sagittal
headlight
by Kayess
products, U.S.

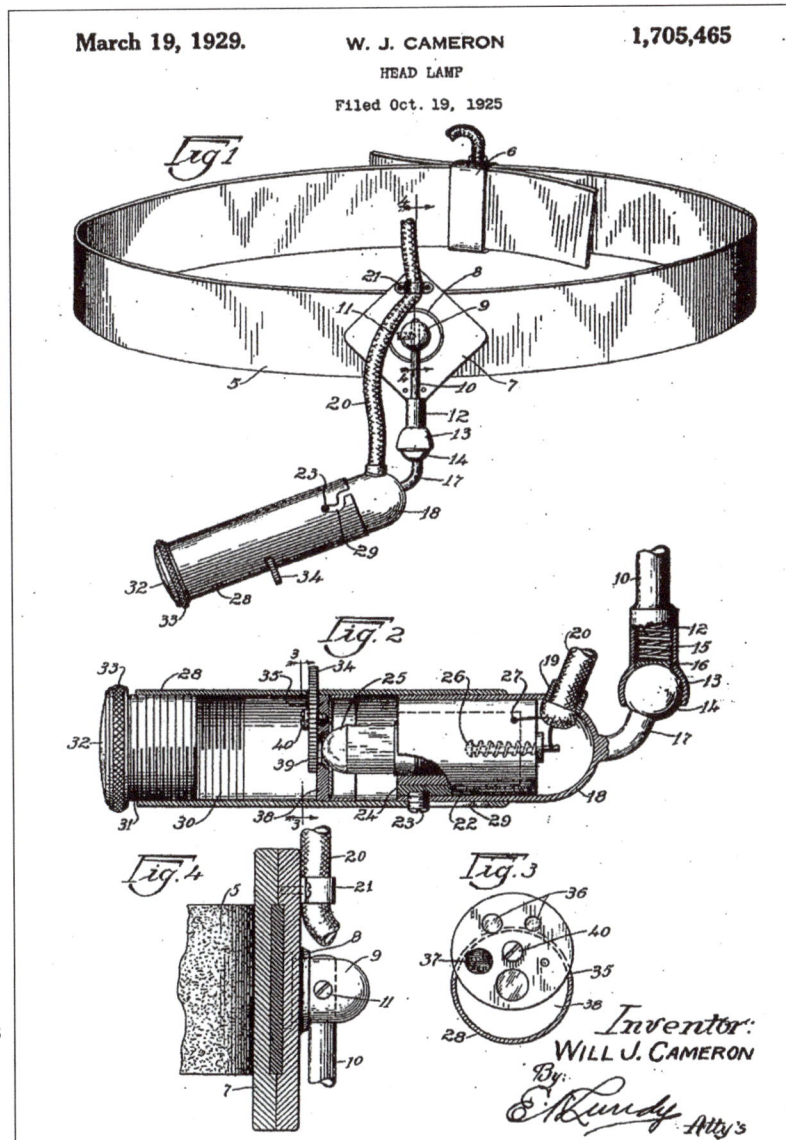

Patent applications
for W.J. Cameron's
headlamp, filed
October 19, 1925.

Stucky's headlight with a large incandescent bulb. Direct illumination is enhanced by a reflective cone.

Early headlight with rheostat. "G.H. Smith, MD" is etched on the strap.

An early light source using a Leviton bulb. The clamp allows it to be positioned to shine directly on the head mirror.

Large headlight with outer ribbon reflective mirror.

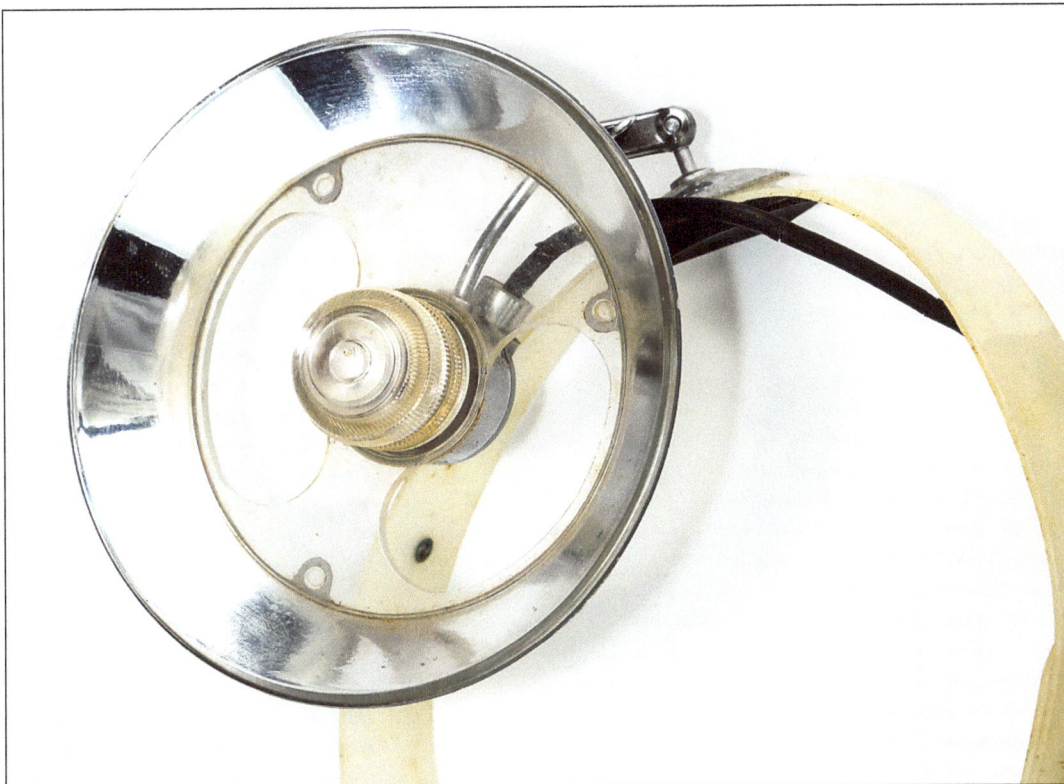

MAGNIFICATION

Proper illumination and direct visualization of the outer ear canal and eardrum are certainly paramount in an otologic examination. However, as Politzer notes, the diagnostic yield becomes much greater with the addition of magnification: "By magnifying the membrana tympani many changes, especially vascular ramifications, small deposits, projections and depressions, movable

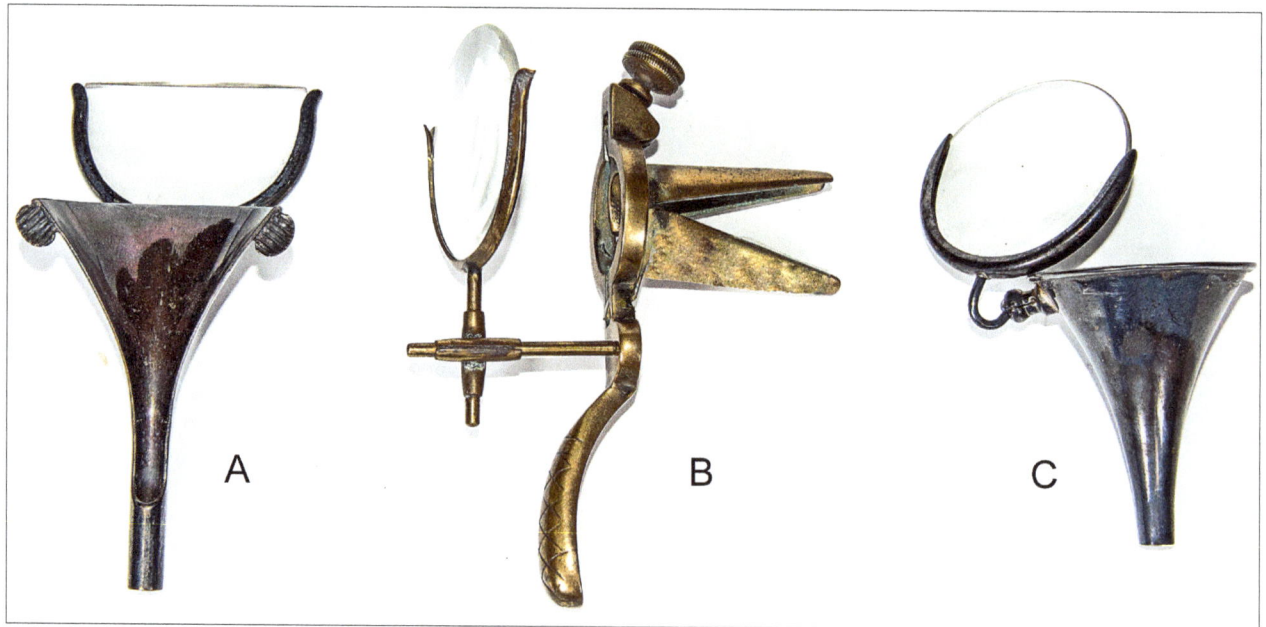

Ear specula with magnifying glasses. A: Modified Auerbach speculum (similar to Voltolini) with half-moon lens and an open speculum for instrumentation, made by Down Bros., London. B: Simrock speculum with exchangeable lens. C: Auerbach speculum with varying magnification powers, made by Maw Son & Thompson of London.

"Arnold and son" Hartmann, ear specula set with magnification lenses.

exudation and air-bubbles in the tympanic cavity, come distinctly into view."[79]

Politzer credits Dr. Auerbach of Hamburg with an early design for a device dedicated to a magnified examination of the ear. "In this speculum," he writes, "the convex lens is fixed by means of a ball-and-socket joint to the outer rim."[80] This description is consistent with some specula in the Touma Medical Museum collection, including one made by Arnold and Sons of West Smithfield, London. This funnel-shaped, circular lumen speculum has a ball-and-socket

joint connecting to a U-shaped piece of metal with a central groove into which magnification lenses of varying powers can be inserted.

A similar speculum made by Down Brothers of London has a U-shaped holder for magnification lenses but also a half-opened speculum with only the tympanic pole being a closed tube. This design allows more light to enter the ear canal and can also accommodate instrumentation. A device made by Simrock around 1860 used the concept of placing a magnifying lens behind a dilating speculum. According to

American trauma surgeon Samuel Gross, this design was actually first contrived by Friedrich Eugen Weber-Liel of Berlin and then improved upon by Simrock, who was from New York. Gross felt this device was the simplest and most efficient way to examine the ear compared to the Toynbee and Wilde specula and Grant's otoscope.[81] The Simrock speculum in the Touma collection confirms this idea of simplicity. It is a bivalve speculum that dilates via a screw mechanism with a small handle. An arm extending from that handle ends at a U-shaped holder for the placement of various magnification lenses.

A device called the ear microscope, created by Weber-Liel, also permitted a magnified view of the ear. The ear microscope had a second purpose as well, described by Henry MacNaughton Jones:

"The purpose of the ear microscope is … to demonstrate the oscillations of the membrane and malleus under normal and abnormal conditions, i.e., to show not only morphological, but also functional alterations with a micrometer. This method of examination is based upon experiments made on the dead body, as follows: If we sprinkle a little starch on the membrana tympani and malleus, and then concentrate the light of a lamp on it by means of a lens, the particles of starch appear as so many bright spots. The sounds of a pipe, or of the human voice, are conveyed through a caoutchouc tube to the external meatus, while the membrane is under observation through a microscope of from 12 to 15 magnifying power. We perceive under the influence of the waves of sound that the starch spots are lengthened into longer or shorter bright lines according to the strength, the height, and the depth of the tones."

The Weber-Liel ear microscope functioned very much like early otoscopes, with a magnifying lens near the eyepiece and a lateral opening with a plane mirror oriented 45° to the long axis of the device. Uniquely, the mirror used in the ear microscope was not perforated; instead, notes Henry Jones in *A Treatise on Aural Surgery*, "the quicksilver coating of the centre of the mirror is removed."[83]

Although many magnification options existed by the start of the 20th century, Politzer maintained that the designs by Brunton and Weber-Liel offered no distinct advantage over the simple lens-behind-an-ear speculum.[84] In his textbook, however, Politzer did describe another magnification device that applied especially to examiners with refractive abnormalities of the eye:

"Persons of normal sight and people short sighted to a moderate degree do not require these lenses. But persons with presbyopia or hypermetropia must positively use convex lenses, as I have found out by experience in my

Allen & Hanburys London head mirror with varying powers of magnification on rotating dial.

classes, for most of them can see the membrane only very indistinctly without a corrective lens, while with one suitable to the degree of the refractive anomaly they not only see the membrane distinctly, but also somewhat magnified. These lenses are best fixed by a contrivance on the back of the mirror."[85]

The contrivance referred to above was a semi-circular piece of vulcanite with a groove into which a lens could be placed. The lens holder was then connected to the rear of the

mirror by a ball-and-socket joint, similar to the magnifying speculum discussed above. For procedures requiring two hands, the mirror could then be placed on a handle or affixed to a headband. A head mirror in the Touma collection uses the same concept, with a convex lens placed behind the central perforation. However, rather than a holder for interchangeable lenses, this mirror incorporates a rotary dial with lenses of differing powers that can be rotated into place as needed. This device is

Sharp & Smith head loupe.

likely to have had more value for ophthalmologists than otologists, but it does demonstrate the similarities between the fields.

The Touma collection also includes magnification goggles that resemble what could be early loupes. One, made by Sharp and Smith of France, can be held in place by an adjustable leather headband. Another, made by Lentz and Sons, has a spring steel headband. Both devices feature enclosed goggles that cover the examiner's eyes and are fitted with binocular magnifying lenses. A similar device by George Tiemann and Company of New York, found in the *Catalogue of Eye, Ear, Nose and Throat Instruments*, is equipped with both magnification goggles and a headlamp.

By the 20th century, nearly all available otoscopes incorporated some sort of magnification lens to aid inspection of the ear canal and eardrum. As otology progressed, offering patients more sophisticated therapeutic options, adaptations had to be made for microsurgeries, necessitating the use of loupes and the creation of the operating microscope.

PRE-ELECTRIC OTOSCOPES

As inventors continued to refine and reimagine already innovative instruments for inspecting the tympanic membrane, they realized that combining an ear speculum, reflective mirror, and source of light in a single device was the next step toward an ideal diagnostic instrument. Two ways of achieving this were explored in the mid-1800s, one of which is more closely associated with the modern otoscope. The other, more rudimentary approach simply used the handle from either a one-piece or bivalve speculum as a point to which reflecting mirrors and light sources could be attached. One of the earliest devices of this nature, developed by Erhard in 1859, combined a one-piece speculum, a centrally perforated mirror, and a wax candle.[102] A similar device created by Weber-Liel, who became a docent in otology at Berlin University, eliminated the candle and added a concentrating lens through which light would pass after being reflected by a mirror with a central opening. Weber-Liel's device also offered the ability to switch the size of speculum.

Camille Miot created two otoscopes similar to Erhard's and Weber-Liel's. One used a plain speculum; the other used a bivalve speculum similar, if not identical, to Lincke's.[103] Blanchet also developed an otoscope with a bivalve speculum and an associated light source, much like the device pictured in J.P. Pennefather's 1873 publication, *Deafness and Diseases of the Ear: The Causes and Treatment*. Finally, in 1867, Charriere made known his otoscope, which Key-Aberg describes as very similar to Blanchet's: "In addition to a bi-partite speculum, fixed in a handle, there was also a concave mirror +/- glasses for accommodation, and a source of light, to which latter there appertained a reflector which

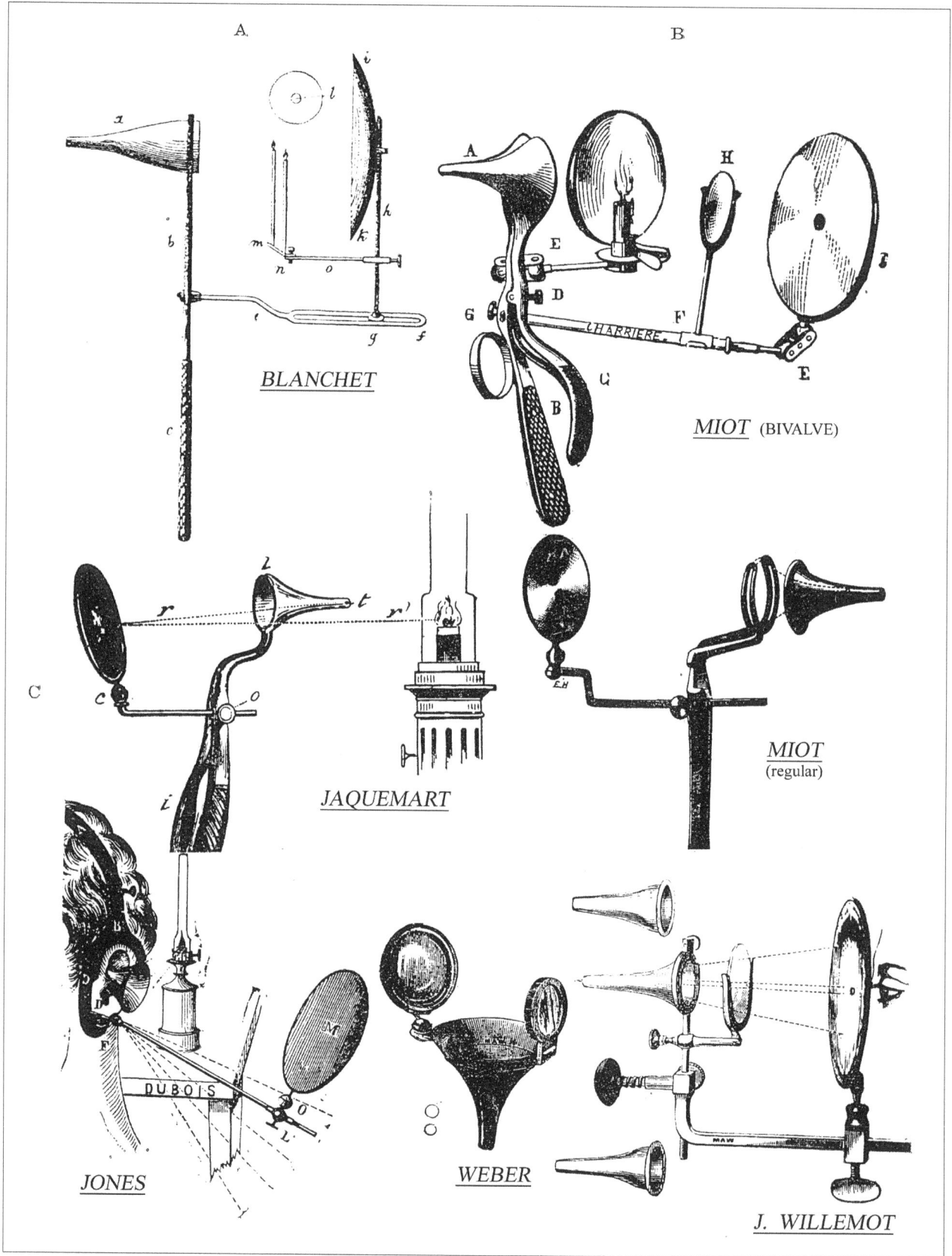

Various early pre-electric otoscopes.

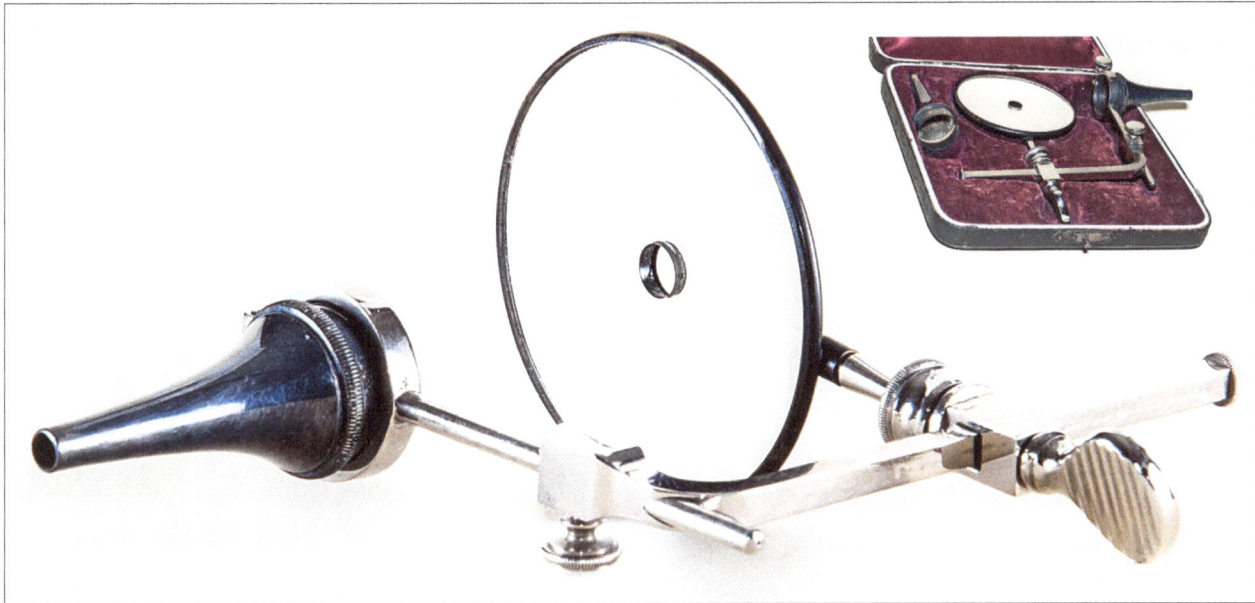

Weber auriscope. This style could be found in medical supply catalogs as late as 1913.

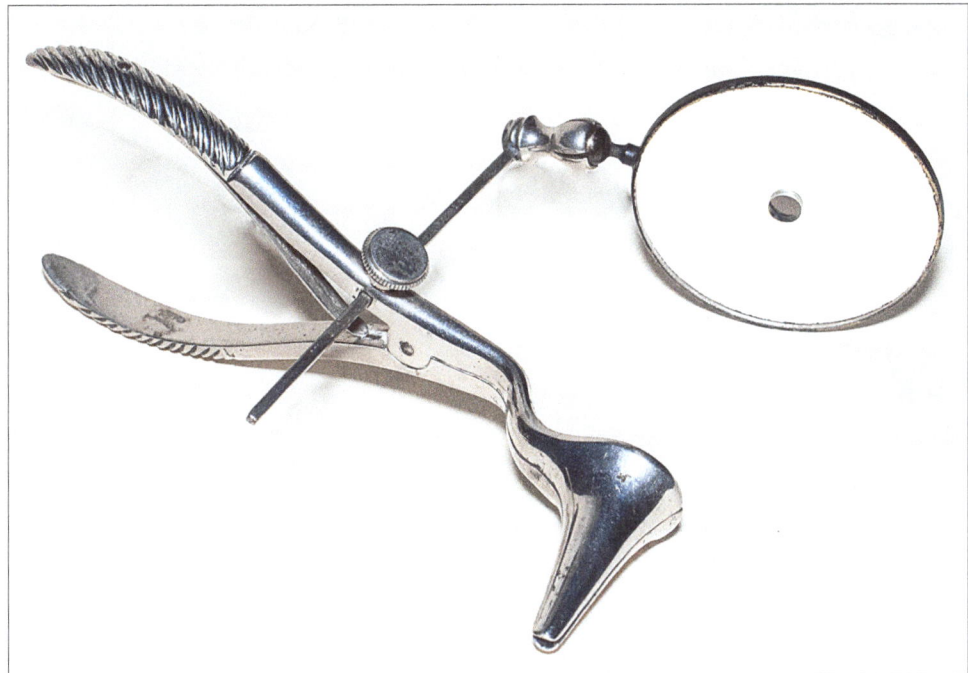

was rotatable in every possible direction."[104]

While one could argue that these designs have some resemblance to more modern, open-frame operating otoscopes, movement toward the diagnostic and operating otoscopes familiar to

Lincke-style bivalve auriscope with Camille Miot speculum.

today's physicians really began in 1834 with an instrument made by Bonnafont: "The design was revolutionary, in that the light source was

placed laterally and by a system of mirrors the light was reflected toward the object, thus making it possible to look straight down the

Hassenstein or Bonnafont otoscope, the same as Brunton's design but without a funnel. The perforated 45-degree mirror reflects the light toward the tip of the speculum.

Hassenstein or Bonnafont otoscope set.

otoscope," writes Neil Weir in *Otolaryngology: An Illustrated History*.[105]

Although Bonnafont's otoscope, like Hofmann's mirror, did not enjoy widespread use or discussion, the concept would survive and be implemented in later devices.

Hassentine improved on Bonnafont's design by introducing a magnifying lens at the eyepiece and interchangeable speculum sizes. The design, conceptually the same as its predecessor, used a cylindrical tube with a lateral opening and a perforated mirror oriented 45° to the long axis of the cylinder.[106] Advances based on this design adopted a funnel-shaped lateral opening to more fully gather light before it struck the mirror. In 1857, otologist Henry Clarke of Newark, New Jersey, developed a device he called "the reflecting otoscope."[107] Clarke claimed that his device could be used during ear surgery, but perhaps

Clarke-Grant otoscope (circa 1860s).

its greater significance was that it was the first instrument of its kind made in America, foreshadowing an eventual shift in the invention and production of otological devices from the European powerhouses to the U.S.

Fellow Newark otologist G. Grant published an otoscope design in the *New York Journal of Medicine* the following year. Grant's design bore a great deal of similarity to Clarke's, as did the otoscope designed by Joseph Toynbee. According to Laurence Turnbull, Toynbee modified Clarke's design to give the funnel portion

Clarke-Grant otoscope with vision tube ending with a magnifying lens.

a wider flange. Staying true to form, Toynbee also used a speculum of his own design with an oval lumen.[108]

The Clarke-Grant otoscope in the Touma collection reveals an interesting design element. The examiner looks through an eyepiece at the back of the otoscope. The opening of this eyepiece is continuous with the lumen of a tube that extends through the central opening of the mirror. The tube terminates at the point where the speculum and larger cylinder join. At this terminus is a magnifying lens that gives the examiner an enlarged view of the ear canal and eardrum. It seems likely that this inner cylinder may interrupt the amount of light that strikes the mirror and is transmitted through the speculum toward the ear canal.

While several otologists had successfully combined the elements of the otoscope before 1865, these devices, according to prolific German otologist Hermann Schwartze, were rarely used by a physician other than the inventor himself.[109] This all changed with John Brunton's 1865 publication, "A New Otoscope or Speculum Auris," in the *Lancet*. The design did not represent a conceptual advancement over its predecessors, but is nonetheless described here in his own words:

"The instrument consists of a brass tube, two inches long and three-quarters of an inch in diameter, to one end of which is made to fit on, by sliding, an ear-piece similar to Toynbee's aural speculum. At the other end is an eye piece, with a lens of moderately magnifying

Brunton otoscope. The 45-degree mirror directs the light beam toward the tip of the ear speculum, and the perforation in the center allows the examiner to have direct view.

Top: Brunton otoscope made by Down Brothers of St. Thomas Street, London, with Wilde speculum. Bottom: Brunton otoscope made by Gowlland, England.

power; the eye-piece slides so as to admit of focal arrangement to suit the eye of the observer. In the body of the instrument, near the ear-piece end, and set at an angle of 45°, is a concave mirror with a hole in the center; this aperture in the mirror is in the line of the axis of the tube and ear-piece. At a right angle to the body of the instrument, and opposite to the mirror, is adapted a sliding funnel-shaped polished silver reflector for collecting and concentrating the rays of light, so that the rays are let in at the side, and, falling on the mirror, are reflected and concentrated into the ear, and carried back to the eye of the observer through, the hole in

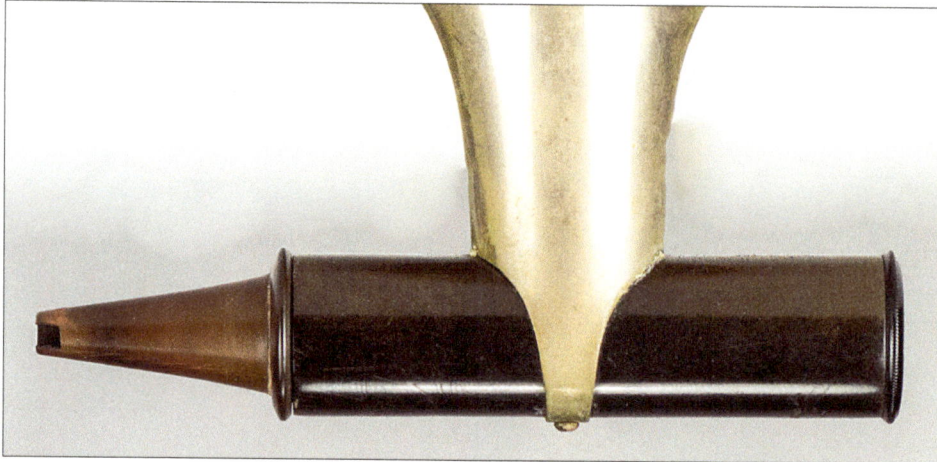

Plastic Brunton auriscope.

and can be turned about to suit either hand of the observer as he may wish."[110]

Brunton, a general surgeon from Glasgow who moved to London to be a medical officer for rail companies, was not a well-known name in otology.[111] However, thanks to the attention generated by its appearance in the *Lancet*, his otoscope became widely used

the mirror, and are magnified by the lens of the eye-piece. There is also a handle attached to the light-reflector, which works on a sliding band,

A: Clarke-Grant otoscope with alcohol lamp light source. B: Clarke-Grant otoscope (for comparison).

across the medical field. Brunton had the device manufactured by optical and mathematical instrument maker James White, who worked for the University of Glasgow. Brunton was actually using this device as early as 1861 and had demonstrated it to the Medical Society of London before publishing his work.[112]

Although instruments of this type would not see widespread use until 1865, there is evidence of a significant advancement in otoscope design only one year after Clarke published his example.

One variation in the Touma collection retains characteristics of the Clarke and Grant designs, but rather than opening into free space to permit light to enter, the lateral opening is connected to an alcohol lamp encased in a metal canister. The lamp is inscribed "H. Leriemodie's patent 1858" and by G. Kellogg of Birmingham, CT." Information on the patent holder is unavailable, but the manufacturer is probably George Kellogg, who had a wide range of interests — from dove-tailing machines, adjustable

Clarke-Grant-style otoscope with adjoined alcohol lamp. The lamp construction is marked: "H. Lerinmondie's Patent 1858, manufactured by A. Kellogg, Birmingham. CT."

Brunton-style auriscope with a candle as a source of light. (See image on the following page.)

obstetrical forceps, and pin manufacturing to various surgical and dental instruments. This design represents a fundamental step toward the modern otoscope in that, for the first time, a speculum, magnification lens, and source of light were combined in a single device. Another otoscope in the collection connects the lateral cylinder to a wax candle. The light strikes a mirror angled at 45°, directing the light beam to the eardrum.

As was common in otoscopy — and in medical instrumentation as a whole — Brunton suggested that the fundamentals of his invention could be adapted for various uses. He claimed, for instance, to have used his otoscope to visualize the nasal passages. Contemporaries and future otologists alike acclaimed Brunton's design for its simple construction and ease of application as well as for the level of detail it revealed to the examiner. Of course, otoscopy

Light from the candle flame is reflected by the 45-degree mirror in the end of the tunnel.

continued to advance from this point, but Brunton's otoscope remained available in major medical supply catalogues into the next century. In another display of longevity, Brunton's design would be the scaffold upon which others continued to develop the otoscope. Most early electric otoscopes incorporated Brunton's design except for the use of a condensing bulb as the light source.

Three years after Brunton published his otoscope, James Hinton, Toynbee's pupil and eventual successor, described an otoscope in *The Medical Times and Gazette* that permitted two clinicians to observe the ear canal simultaneously.

Called the "Demonstrations-Auriscope,"[113] Hinton's device followed Brunton's basic design, but positioned two eyepieces at right angles and fixed a light source to the lateral opening. Brunton felt this device was too similar in design to his own to go without mention and was confident in the ease with which a novice could use his otoscope. He made this known in a letter to the editor of *The Medical Times and Gazette*:

"Now, if Mr. Hinton and your readers will have the kindness to look at the 617th page of the *Lancet* for December 2, 1865, they will there find that Mr. Hinton's so-called new instrument

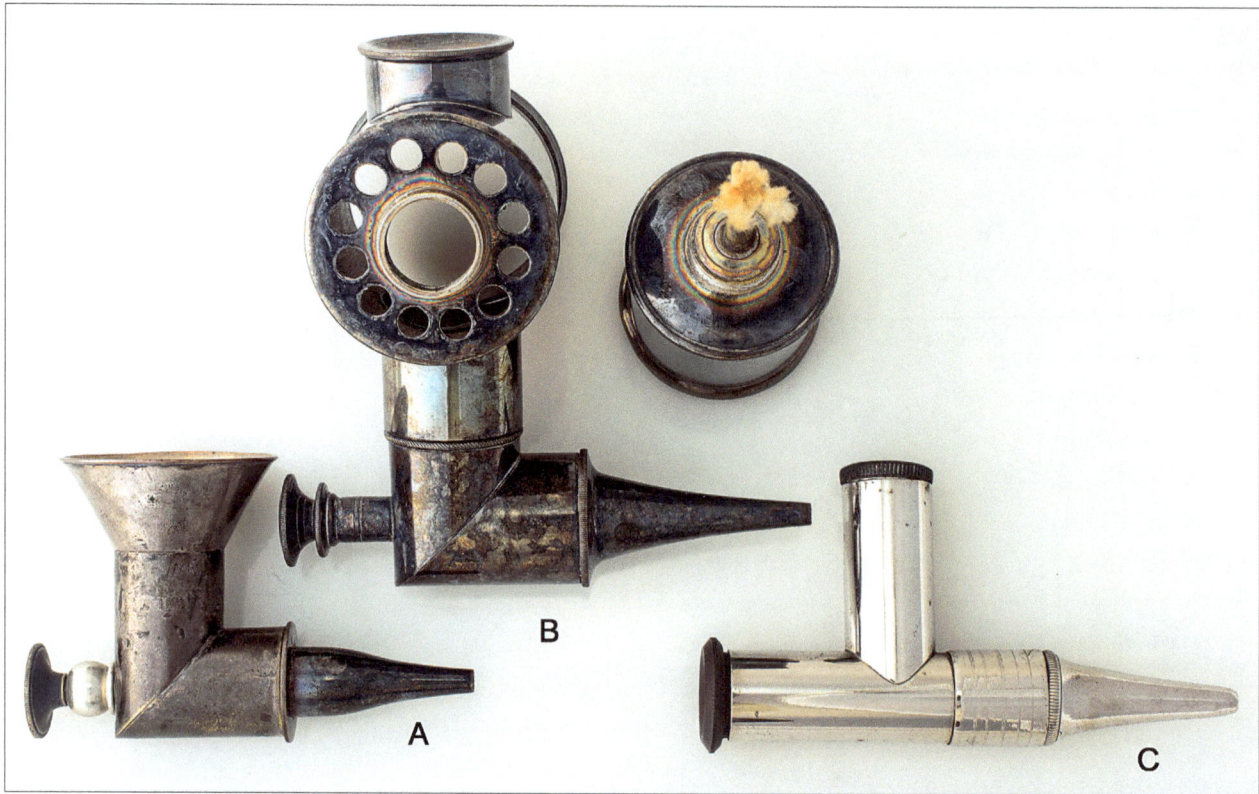

The progression of lighting in Brunton otoscopes. A: Clarke-Grant-style auriscope. B: Clarke-Grant-style otoscope with alcohol lamp attachment. C: Brunton-style otoscope with the application of electric illumination.

has been invented and described by me[.] ... I have never had any difficulty in demonstrating the membrane, etc., to a second or third person, as one or two trials will enable any one with ordinary capabilities to master the use of the otoscope, and thereby to see for himself."[114]

Knowingly or not, Hinton had made use of the construction already described by Brunton and Bonnafont. Additionally, an otoscope intended for teaching purposes had already been developed by Professor August Lucae of Berlin in 1860. As Key-Aberg writes, "It consisted of a centrally perforated plane mirror which, during investigation — in which operation, sunlight could, of course, be employed — served both as a reflector and a demonstrator of the drum of the ear. In the plane mirror the second observer could, if he occupied a suitable position relative to the teacher and the source of light, without any great difficulty catch an inverted picture of the illuminated membrane."[115]

Exemplified by Lucae's and Hinton's teaching otoscopes, plane mirrors, in theory, could be used *ad infinitum* to redirect an image of the tympanic membrane in as many directions as desired. Emil Siegle applied this concept in 1874 to invent a device that allowed him to inspect his own tympanic membrane.[116]

Voltolini further modified Brunton's otoscope in 1873 by making it a pneumatic device. He also made available the option of a speculum with a lateral opening. With this modification, Voltolini created one of the earliest models of an operating otoscope.[117] In fact, this design created a cross between an operative and a diagnostic otoscope — something companies like Welch Allyn continue to produce and improve upon to this day.

In 1894, Englishman Thomas Mark Hovell addressed two issues he'd experienced with the Brunton otoscope. Hovell felt that not enough light entered through the lateral opening, so he redesigned the lateral funnel to allow more light into the cylinder. Secondly, he felt the eyepiece did not allow convenient adjustment for focusing. He thought this could be improved by attaching the lens to a movable eyepiece.[118] Even though Hovell felt these were necessary modifications, others remained satisfied with the existing Brunton design.

All the aforementioned otoscopes required the examiner to look through the lens with one eye, thereby limiting depth perception. Emilio de Rossi, professor of otology in Rome and Paris, and Adolf Eysell addressed this with the inventions of binocular otoscopes in 1872 and 1873, respectively. Politzer gives the following description and assessment of these devices:

"E. de Rossi has constructed a binocular otoscope, which consists of a plane glass plate, fixed to a frontal band, from which the rays of the sun are reflected into the meatus. Eysell recommends for binocular inspection two prisms of a small refractive angle (3°-5°), which are inserted between the reflector and the speculum. By this contrivance the observer gets a transverse double view, which after some practice will melt into one. The binocular inspection of the membrane is, however, of little advantage to the expert, while difficulties are created for the inexperienced observer by the great distance from the object with [d]e Rossi's instrument, and by having to combine the transverse views of the membrane obtained with Eysell's prisms into one image."[119]

Burnett agreed with Politzer's assessment of de Rossi's device, saying, "The distance of the eye from the membrana tympani, thirty centimetres, necessary to obtain a binocular view, renders the instrument of no very great practical utility."[120] Thus, Brunton's design remained the standard for conventional, non-electric otoscopes. During the next phase of otoscopy, inventors would continually revisit its design elements in developing electric otoscopes.

ELECTRIC OTOSCOPES

Otologists were not the first to use incandescent bulbs to inspect the body's concavities. Maximilian Nitze of Vienna introduced the first endoscope using incandescent illumination in 1887. Much of Nitze's early work in the infancy of endoscopy was done in cooperation with Viennese instrument maker Josef Leiter.[121] Also in 1887, Leiter created a panelectroscope, an example of which is in the collection at the Touma Medical Museum. This device shares many features with operating otoscopes, and it is tempting to think it might have provided inspiration to other instrument designers.

The next significant design advancement came in the 1890s with the work of K. Schall and Pedro Verdos. Schall was the first to place

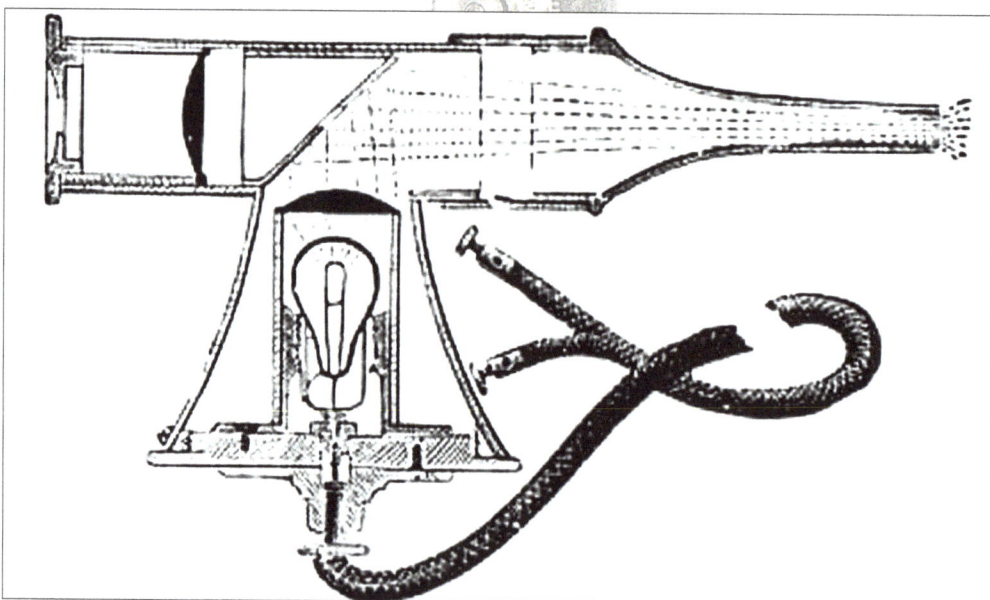

Early electric Brunton otoscope in 1905 Schall & Sons, Ltd. supply catalog. An incandescent light bulb replaced natural light.

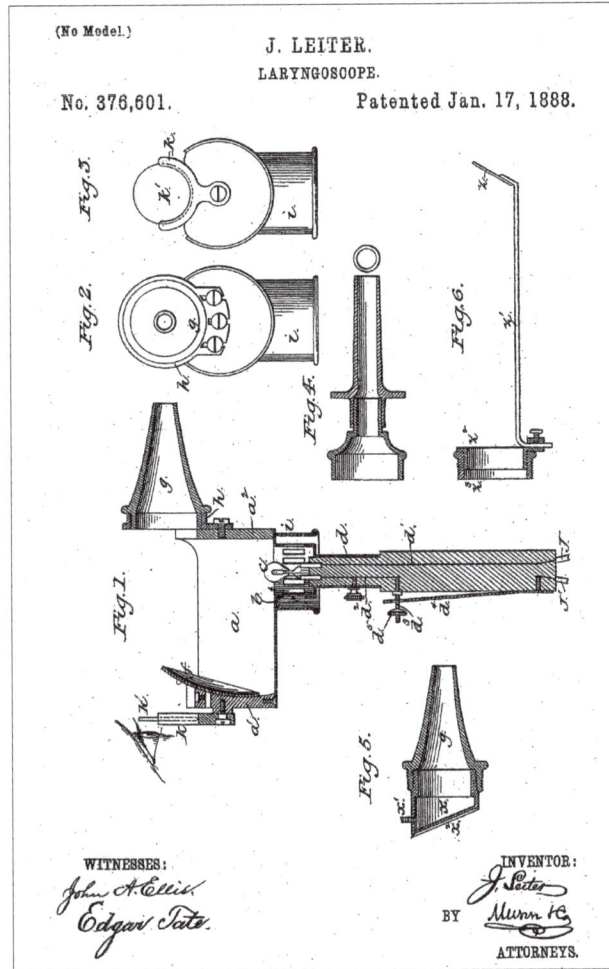

Patent application for J. Leiter's "Laryngoscope,"
January 17, 1888.

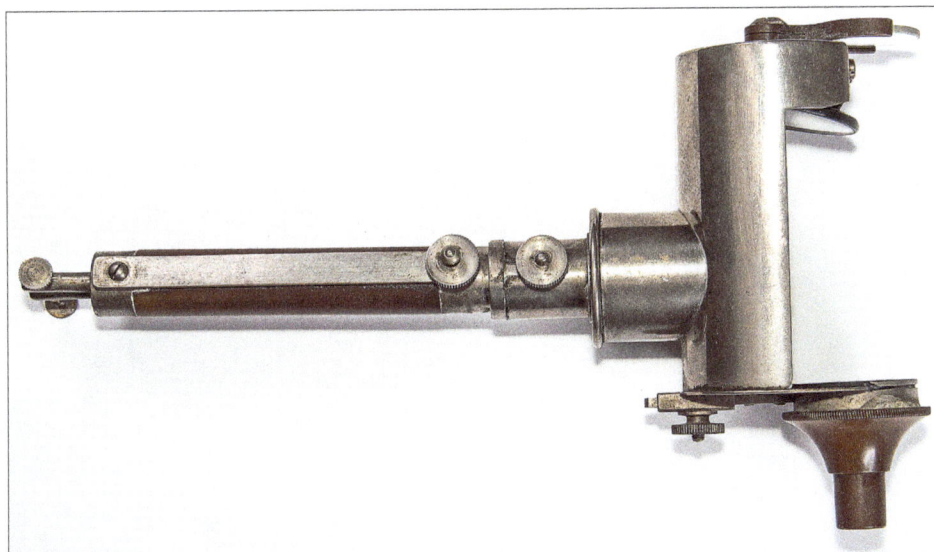

Josef Leiter panelectroscope, designed by the Viennese instrument maker in
1887. It is the first to have all the components of the modern otoscope.

an electric lamp in the lateral opening of a Brunton-type otoscope.[122] Verdos, of Barcelona, added a six-volt lamp in 1895 for more powerful illumination.[123] Their devices represented significant movement toward the modern otoscope. In essence, an electric light source redirected toward the tympanic membrane, changeable specula, and a magnification lens for the observer describes otoscopes being made well into the 20th century. A device in the Touma collection fits this description very well: an electric-powered device fundamentally the same as Brunton's with an incandescent bulb as the light source directed at the centrally perforated mirror within the otoscope's main cylinder. The eyepiece at the back, like nearly all otoscopes at this point, features a magnification lens. This same design appeared in the 1901 Wm. H. Armstrong and Co. catalogue, along with conventional and battery-powered Brunton models. With the invention of these devices and others like them, otologists and

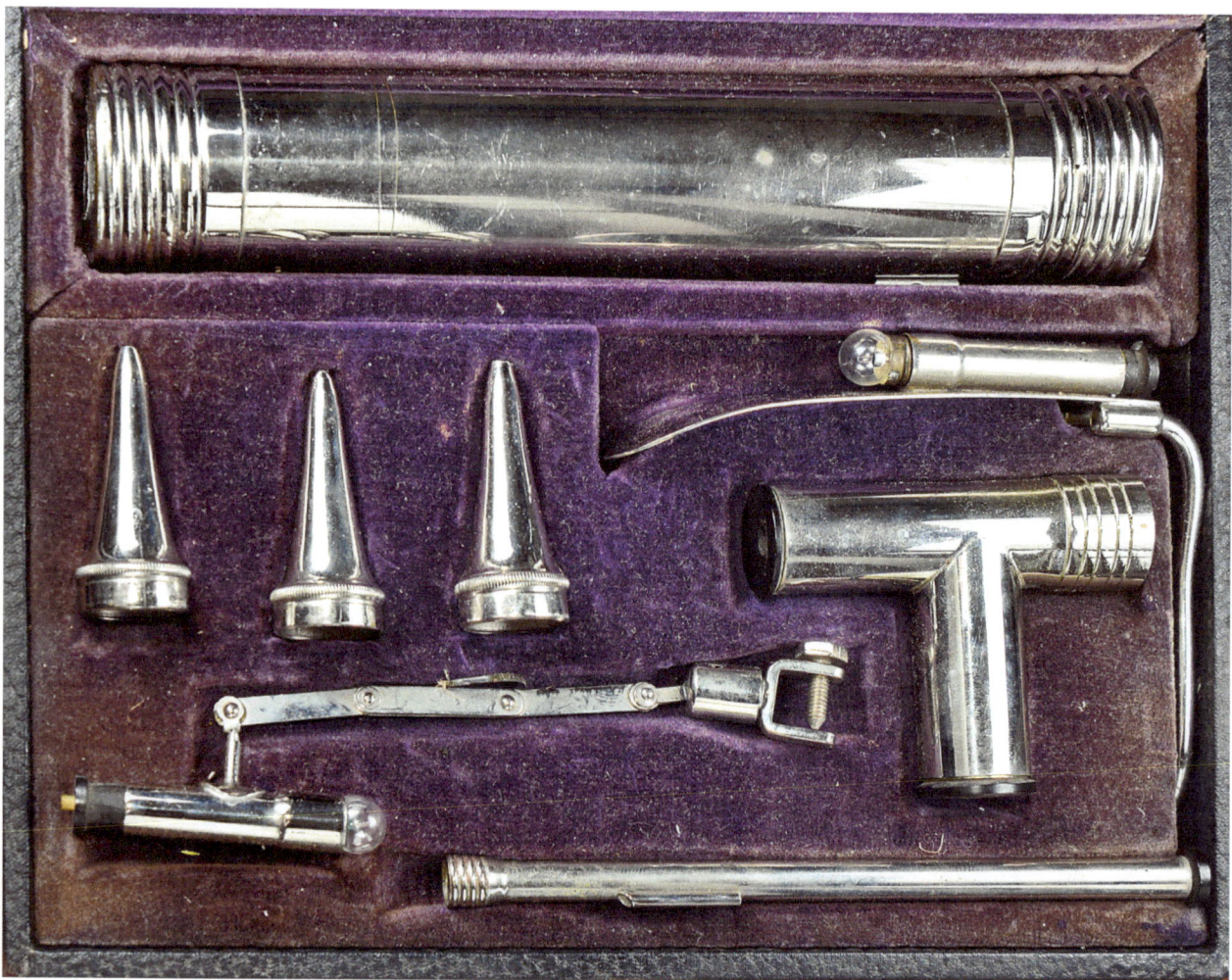

Verdos otoscope: Very early battery-operated Brunton-type otoscope set.

their patients could benefit from the convenience of an electric light applied directly to the otoscope. This advantage allowed examination with the consistency of an electrically powered light and little to no heat being transferred to the patient, and it required no changes in position to optimally capture an ambient light source. The only fundamental differences between these early electric devices and those made later in the 1900s are the power supply and the positioning of the light source. The design features dictated largely by the sizes and types of electric lights available at the time. From this point, electric otoscopes would develop hand in hand with advances in electricity and lighting, like the development of the electric headlamp. In this progression, certain common design challenges arose consistently, most notably positioning the light source so it did not obstruct the clinician's view and directing the light so its path paralleled the line of sight, thereby achieving the most effective illumination.

Very early battery-operated Brunton-type otoscope (circa 1910).

The Brunton otoscope and its electric versions rely on light redirected through a perforated mirror and, by convention, do so in closed cylinders. The next level in advancing otoscope design would involve the use of redirected light without need for perforation in a mirror and opening the device such that the ear canal could be visualized and instruments could be used simultaneously. Schall produced one of the earliest electric open-frame operating otoscopes around 1896. Another otoscope that exemplifies the progression in redirected

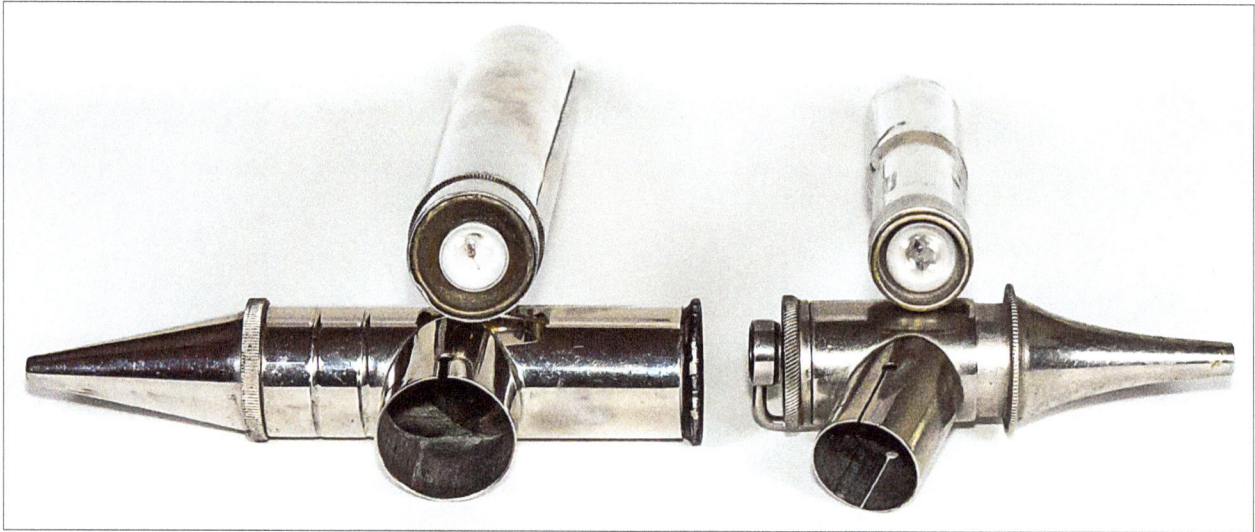

(Left) First-generation Brunton-type electric otoscope. (Right) Modern-looking Typhoo medical torch otoscope. Both use the same type of incandescent bulbs and perforated reflective mirrors.

light is the "Typhoo" Medical Torch, a battery-powered device with an incandescent bulb that sits at the end of a shaft upon which the device can be fixed. The instrument head has an angled plane mirror in its base that takes up roughly a third of the view from the back of the scope. An eyepiece with magnification and an ear speculum on the other side complete this simple design. While this was not one of the first battery-powered otoscopes, the introduction of batteries as a power source deserves mention, as it made house calls easier and permitted examinations to proceed without the hassle of a tailing power cord.

The Touma collection has several

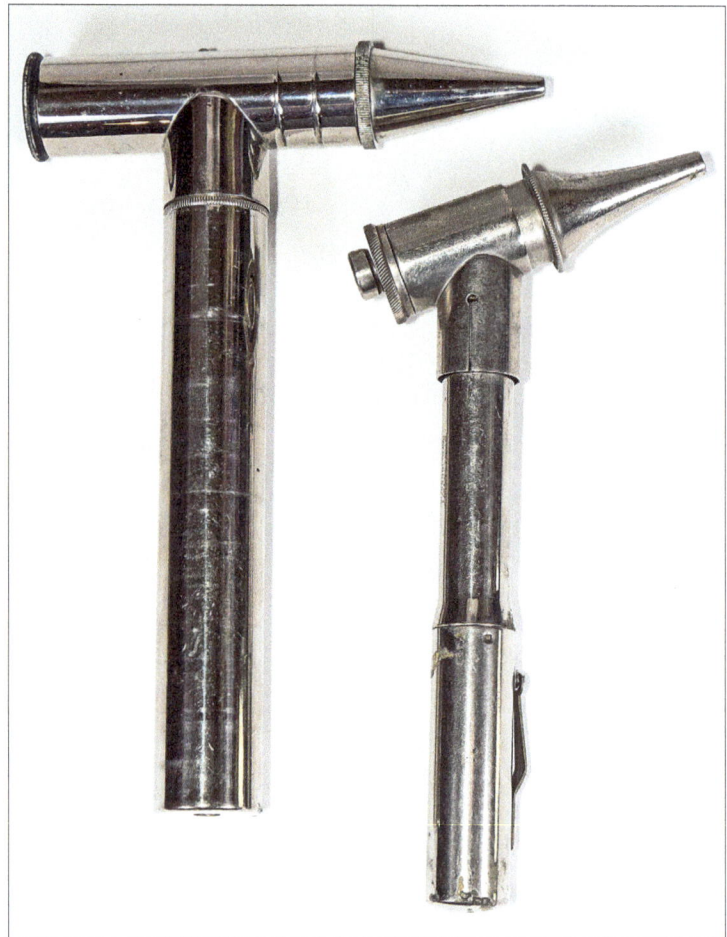

(Left) Brunton-type electric otoscope. (Right) Typhoo medical torch otoscope with Eveready batteries.

battery-powered otoscopes that stand out in terms of their compact size and simplicity. The "De Lyte Surgeon," made by Pennsylvania Surgical Manufacturing Company in 1917, comes in a small leather carrying case. The small metal handle houses the batteries and has attachment sites where the magnification lens and speculum holder can be held in place. The design is focused more on portability and ease of use than factors such as optimal line of sight relative to the axis of the light and speculum tip. Nonetheless, it's apparent that this device could function well in the bag of a traveling physician or even in the pack of a field medic in a military setting. The equally compact "Cavascope" is very similar. It does not feature a magnification lens but does achieve illumination by way of a large incandescent bulb with a built-in convex lens to concentrate the light.

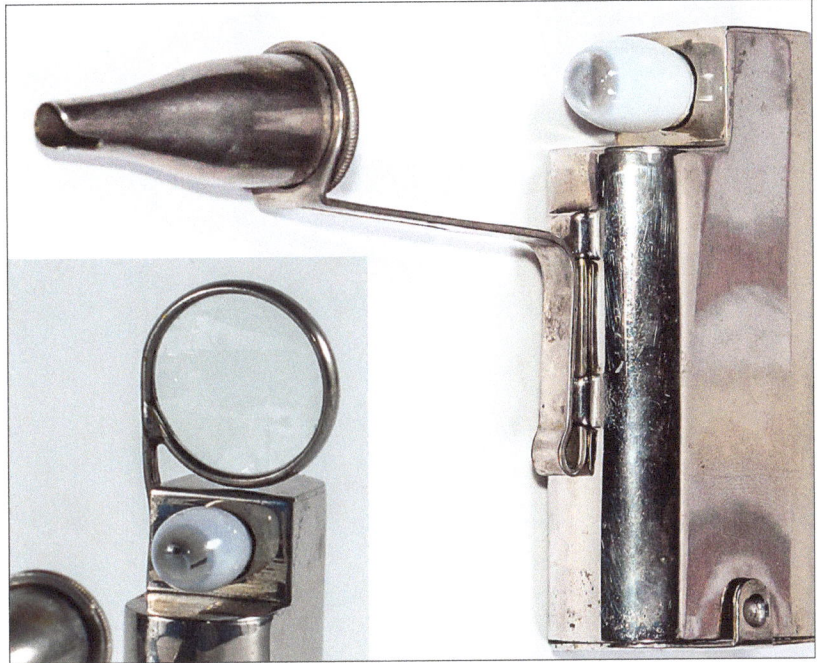

De Lyte Surgeon otoscope (patent June 12, 1917) with incandescent bulb, built-in lens and removable magnifyling lens.

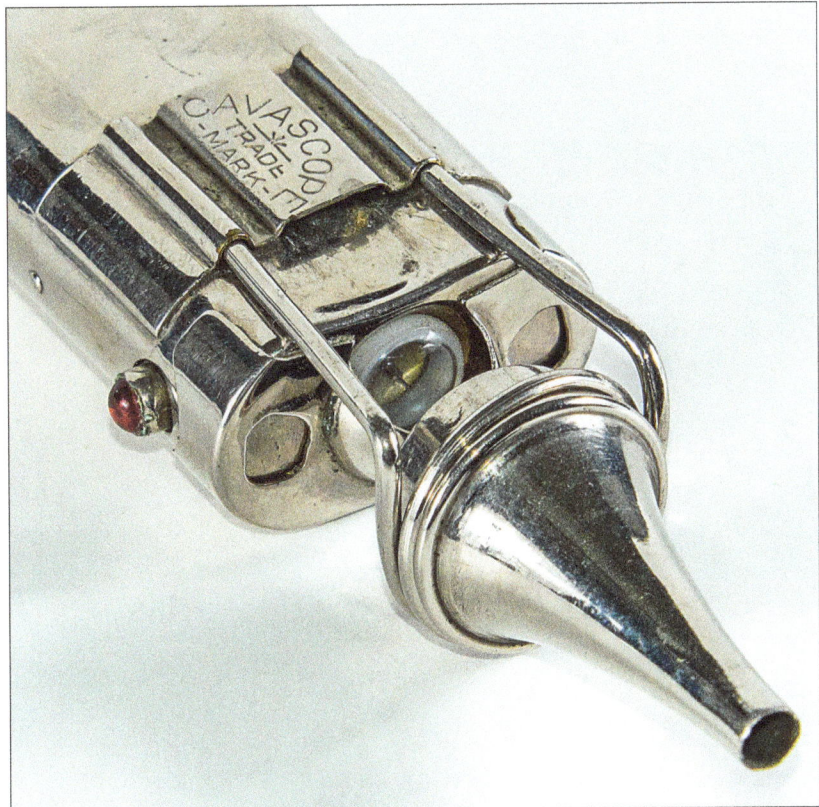

Battery-powered Cavascope.

One of the earliest battery-operated otoscopes is the Davidson and Company otoscope. It has a manual contact switch to turn it off and on. The light bulb is considered one of the earliest that has a condensing lens; however, the bulb is much larger than the next generation of light bulbs. The light source is a large "Davon" dry battery located in the otoscope box. The Royal battery-powered otoscope in the Touma collection demonstrates the early difficulties in directing the light beam toward the eardrum; much of the visual field is obstructed by the top

A Davidson & Co. otoscope with Erhard speculum. The arrow points to the manual off and on contact switch.

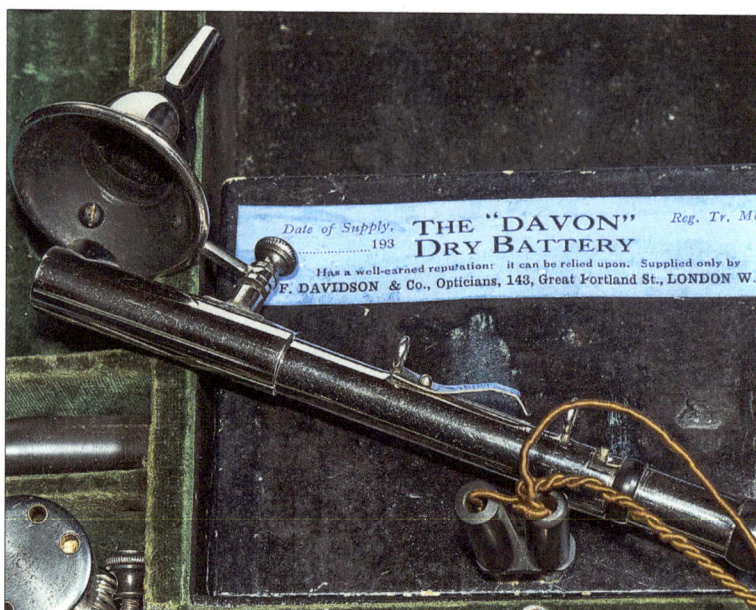

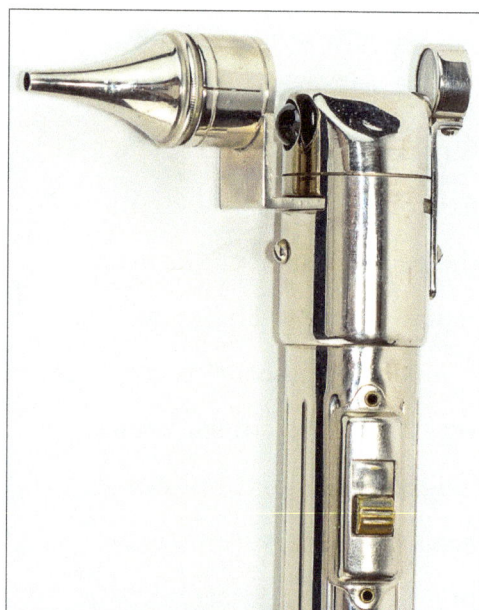

(Left) F. Davidson & Co. otoscope powered by "Davon dry battery (circa 1920). (Right) Royal battery-powered otoscope (circa 1915). This device demonstrates the early difficulties of providing direct illumination, as much of the visual field is obstructed by the top of the handle which houses the light bulb.

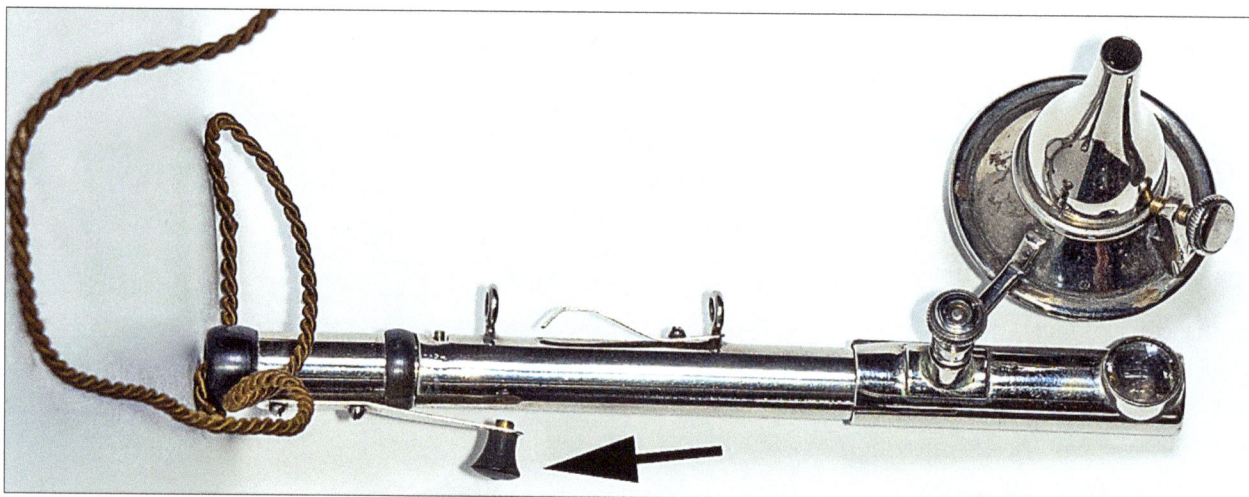

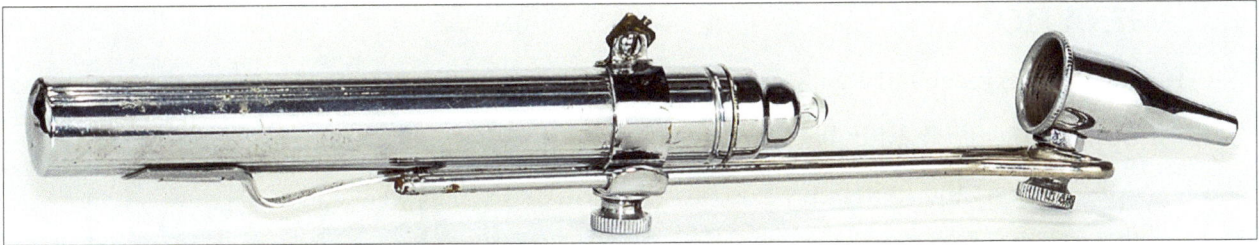

C.W. Wolff (Surgeon X-L-Lyte, $15.00, November 19, 1931) pocket otoscope in operational mode. The speculum holder can be used as a tongue blade.

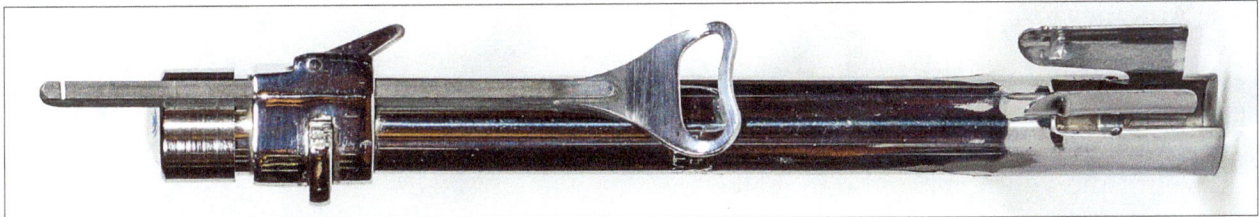

C.W. Wolff otoscope in storage mode.

of the battery housing. The C.W. Wolff otoscope in the collection is another important development of the modern otoscope. It does not have a magnifying lens, but it is versatile; one of its components is a tongue blade which can also serve as a platform to insert the ear speculum.

As the otoscope continued in its advancement, several challenges needed to be addressed, including the alignment of the line of vision and the light beam with magnification. The other challenge was creating a versatile otoscope that could be diagnostic and operative when needed. Electricity solved many problems by providing better illumination, but technical difficulties remained.

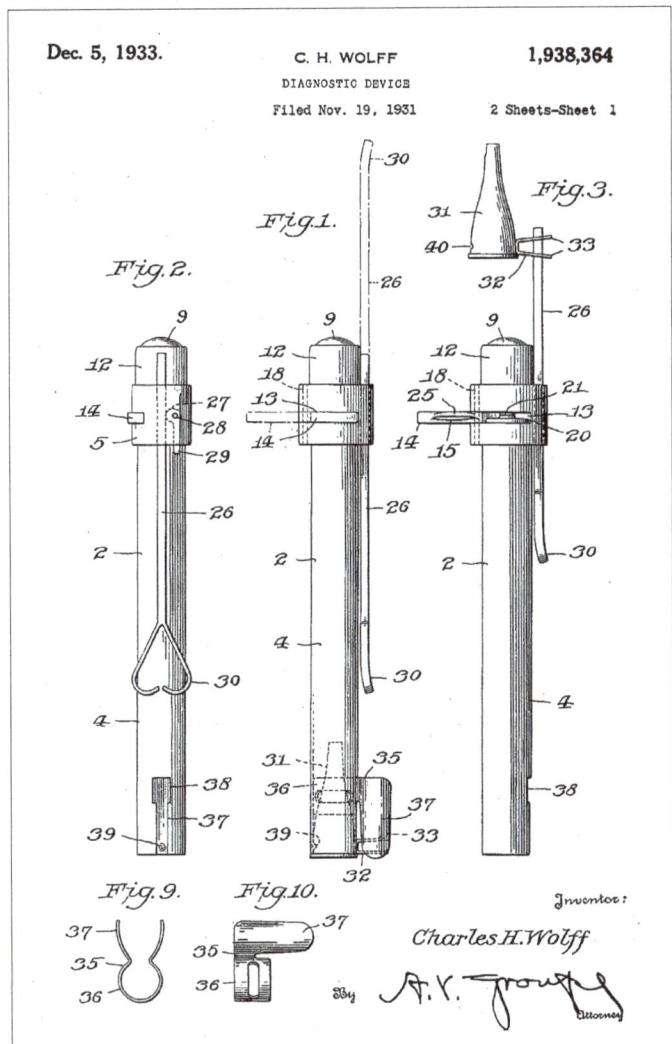

Patent application of C.H. Wolff's "Diagnostic Device," November 19, 1931

ILLUMINATION

After adopting electricity as a source of light, simple mid-sized light bulbs were used in otoscopes such as the Leiter, Typhoo, and Brunton designs. Light from these bulbs shone in all directions, causing glare and dim light. The Aurolite otoscope used the hood concept, covering the entire bulb except for a window in the front to reduce the glare of the light bulb. However, the light remained dim. Later, the same light bulbs were used, but they were covered with a plastic hood and lens to condense the light beam. The Touma ENT Museum has several examples of this modification, including early National and Welch Allyn otoscopes. The hood with the lens was eventually discarded,

Lighting of the AUROLITE otoscope consists of a simple incandescent bulb in a domed housing.

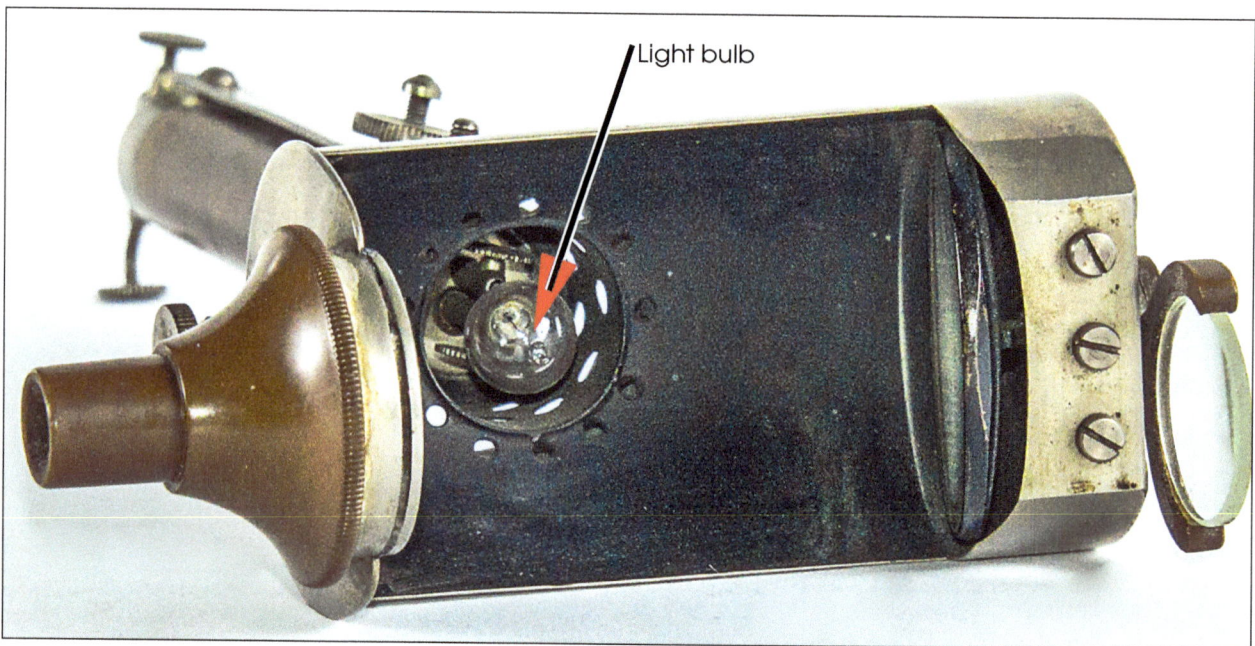

Light bulb

Leiter panelectroscope with a magnifying glass and reflective mirror on the right side and a small incandescent light in the center.

Two otoscopes dating from the 1920s and 1930s with regular incndescent bulbs and hoods with condensing lenses. (Left) National otoscope. (Right) Welch Allyn otoscope.

and a new generation of smaller light bulbs with built-in condensing lenses were used.

One of the more widely used electric models, made by the Wappler Electric Manufacturing Company of New York, appears in many textbooks from around 1910, including Gorham Bacon's 1913 *Manual of Otology*.[124] This device is quite significant in that it was one of the first to use direct illumination. This Wappler otoscope is wall-powered, which provides electricity to the small bulb that sits in a housing just behind a metal ring that holds the ear speculum. At the

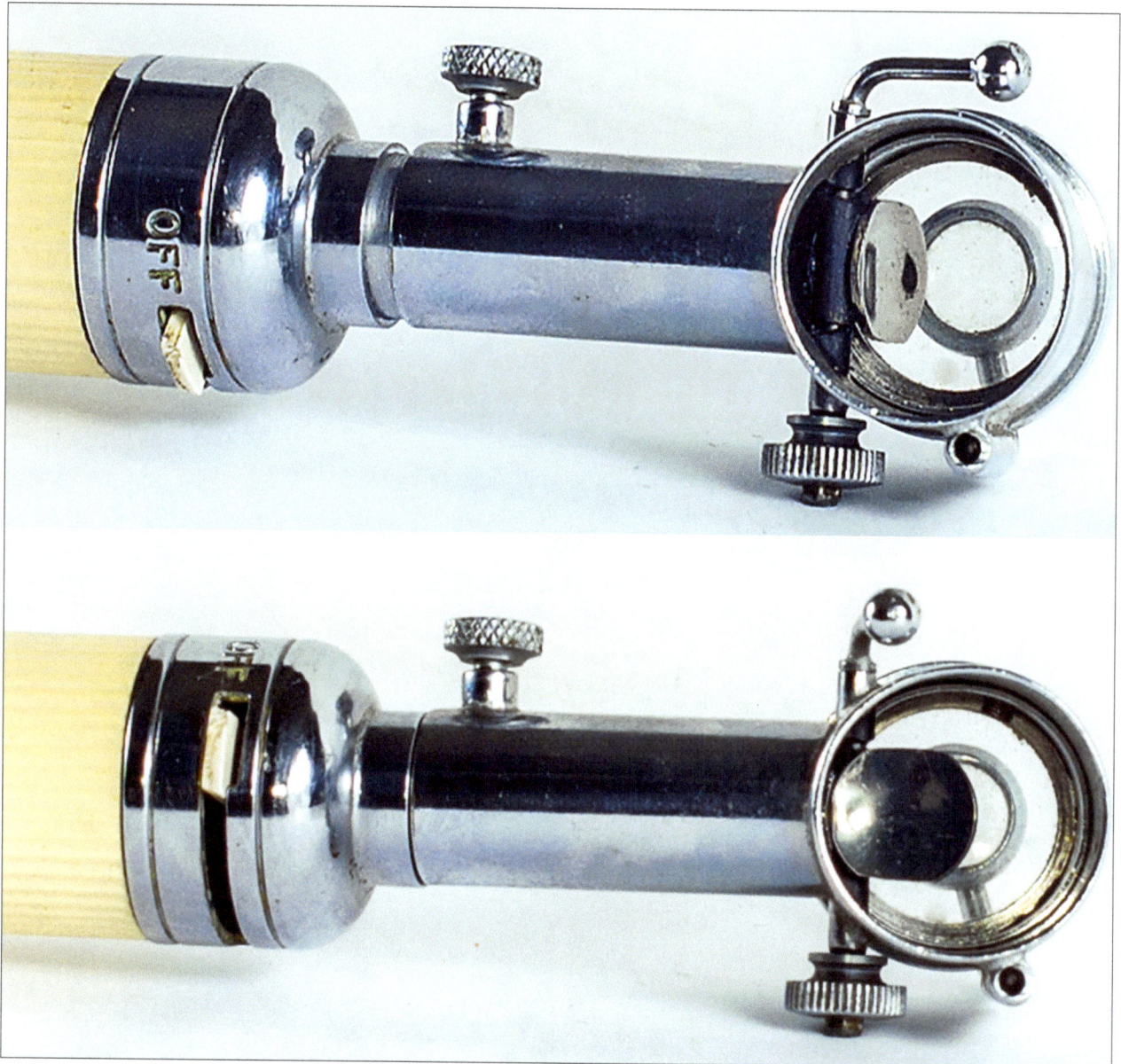

Phillip Harris, Ltd. otoscope with hinged mirror. The angle of the mirror can be adjusted to direct the light to the center of the speculum; however, doing so may occlude part of the visual axis.

end of the housing is a convex lens that concentrates the light, and behind that housing is a magnifying lens on a swinging arm that can be brought in and out of view as needed. With this open design, the 1910 Wappler could conceivably have been used for operative purposes.

National Electric made another operating otoscope, essentially the same as those described above, that began to look more like the ones in use today, thanks largely to the use of a smaller light bulb. The speculum was held in place by a metal ring, and a magnifying lens sat opposite the speculum; a small incandescent bulb was positioned between them. The light sat inside a small plastic housing with a single opening facing the speculum. A convex lens condensed the light into a strong beam that was projected forward through the speculum. National Electric's design embodies the simple fundamentals of an operating otoscope; only a few more improvements in illumination would be needed to incorporate all the elements of today's operating otoscopes.

An otoscope made by British supply company Philip Harris Limited displays characteristics of a device outfitted for diagnostic purposes, such as two magnification lenses and a sealable instrument head with an aperture for a rubber hose. The interesting thing about this otoscope is the illumination mechanism. Like other devices of the early 20th century, it relies on light reflected by a concave mirror; however, in this case, the mirror sits in the floor of the instrument head and is attached to a hinge. This hinge is controlled by a handle on the outside of the instrument head and can be locked in place by a nut on the opposite side, allowing the examiner to adjust the light's projection.

In 1929 another attempt to provide effective illumination in an operating otoscope without obstructing the examiner's view was made by inventor William Patterson of Rochester, New York, who was assignor to Bausch & Lomb.[125]

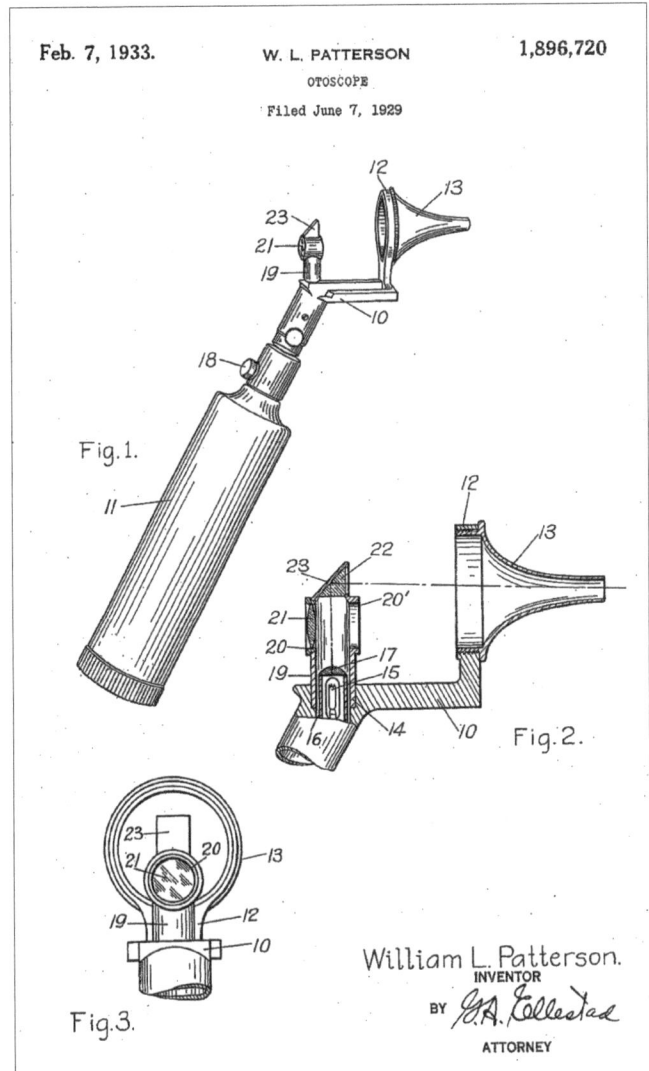

Patent application for W.L. Patterson's "Otoscope," June 7, 1929, (light bulb with prism).

Patterson created a casing that fit over a simple incandescent lamp with a carrying lens, much like the National Electric models. Patterson's design allowed light to travel past the examiner's line of sight before being redirected toward the speculum by means of a prism. This gave the otoscopist an unobstructed view; however, the line of sight was thereby situated slightly below the level of the tip of the speculum and

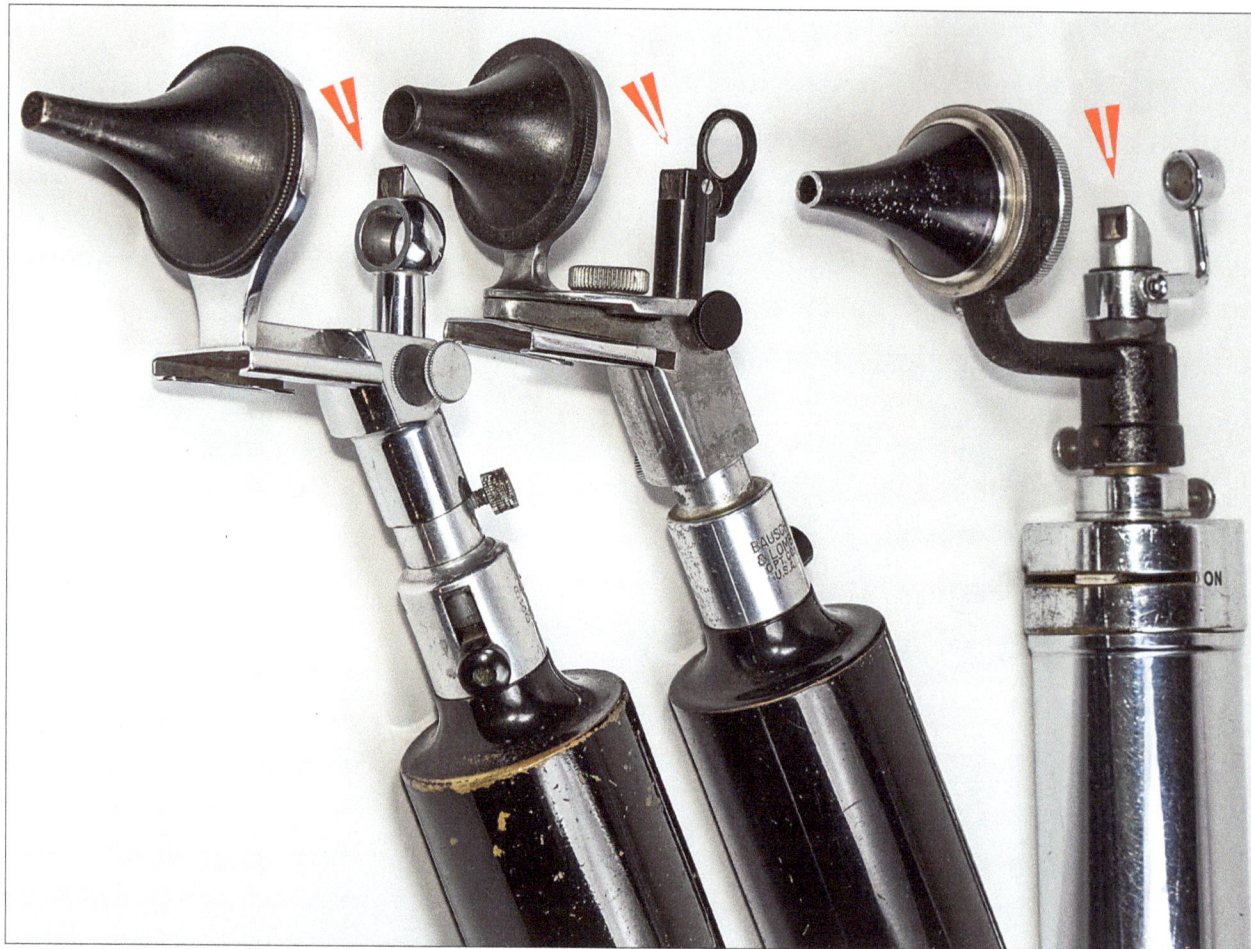

Three Bausch & Lomb otoscopes wtih a prism, marked by the arrows, to direct light to the center of the speculum.

the trajectory of the light. The Touma collection has three Bausch & Lomb otoscopes with prism lighting.

While otoscopes with a light source in the field of view provided satisfactory illumination, innovations in light transmission allowed inventors to overcome the visual obstruction. In 1940, fiber optic bundles were placed in a variety of surgical instruments to illuminate body cavities.[131] By moving the light source itself out of the field of view, more powerful lamps could be used, providing brighter light without further obstructing the physician's line of sight. William C. Moore and John D. Connors, working for Welch Allyn, began to apply this concept around 1960 by integrating fiber optic bundles into the sidewalls of a diagnostic otoscope's distal tip. They explain the advantages of this design in their 1964 patent claim:

"The principal objective of the present invention, accordingly, is to provide a speculum, for diagnostic instruments which have a light source, having an unobstructed viewing passage therethrough, and, at the same time, having light transmitting means capable of increased light emission which uniformly illuminates the field to be viewed."[132]

Several years later, fiber optics would be applied to a dedicated operating otoscope, as outlined in a 1977 patent claim by Moore, Connors, and Richard W. Newman, which also

mentions a newer light source: the halogen lamp.

"[T]he light is whiter and more uniform than the light output of prior art instruments. To obtain more light, a larger than normal lamp is employed which preferably is a halogen lamp as the latter gives a whiter light than a vacuum lamp and has a longer life span. Since a larger lamp produces more heat and would be more of an obstruction if positioned in the

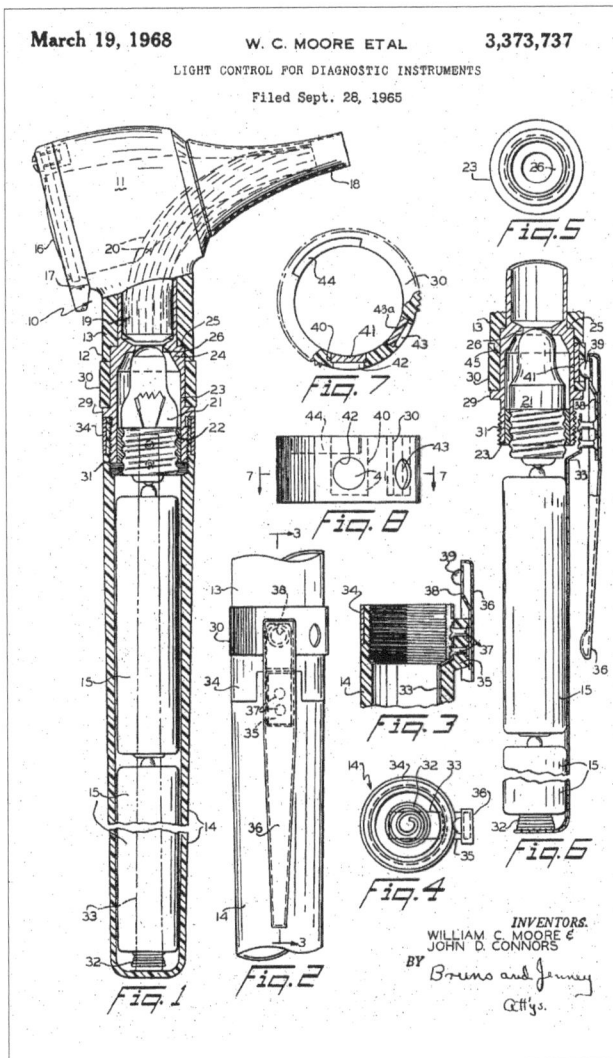

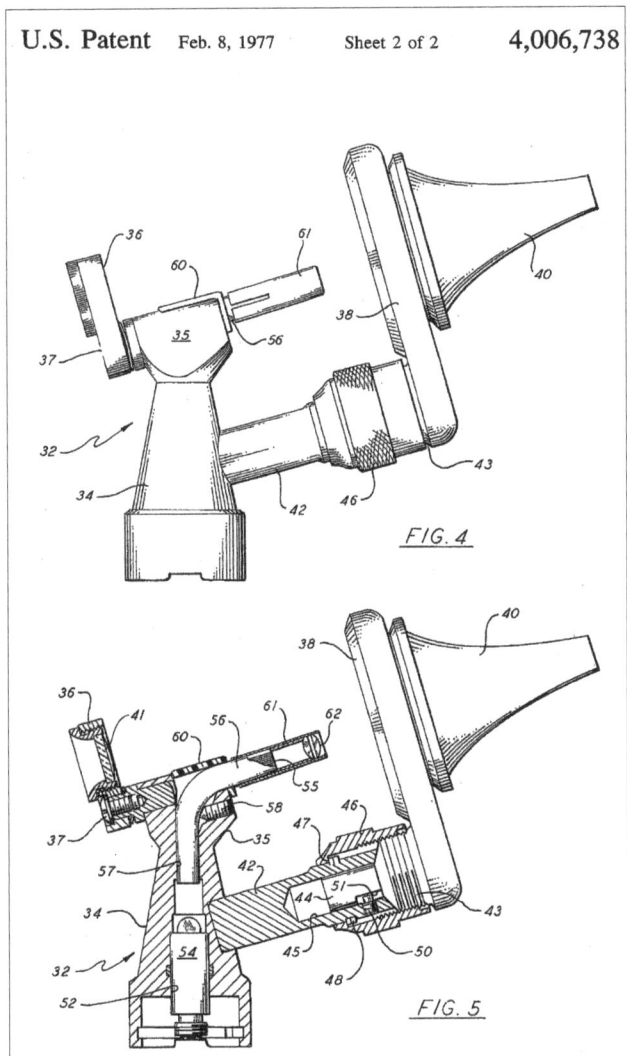

((Left) Patent application for W.C. Moore's, et al, "Light Control for Diagnostic Instrument" (fiberoptic light), September 28, 1965. (Right) Patent application #4,006,738 "Halogen Lamps with Fiber Optic Filaments", February 8, 1977.

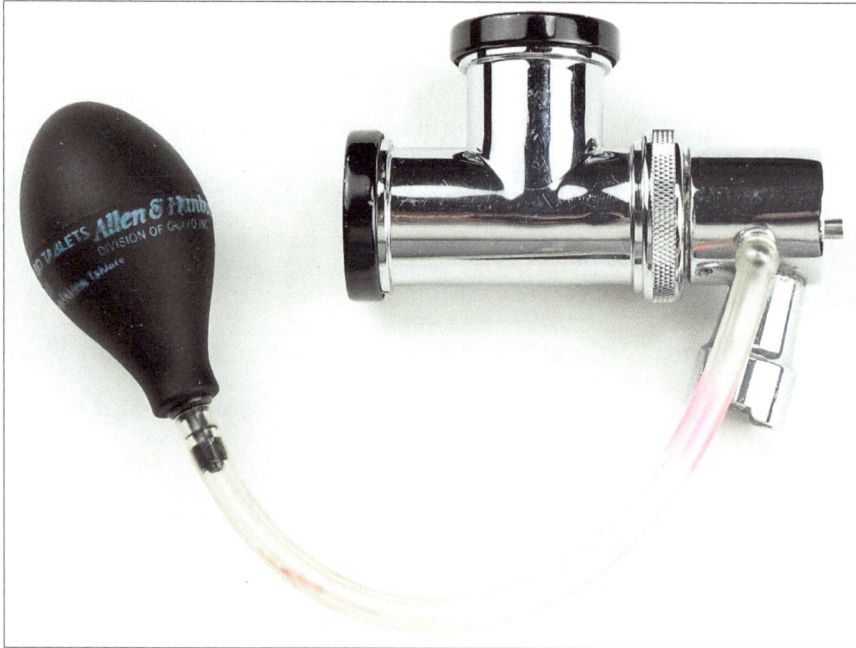

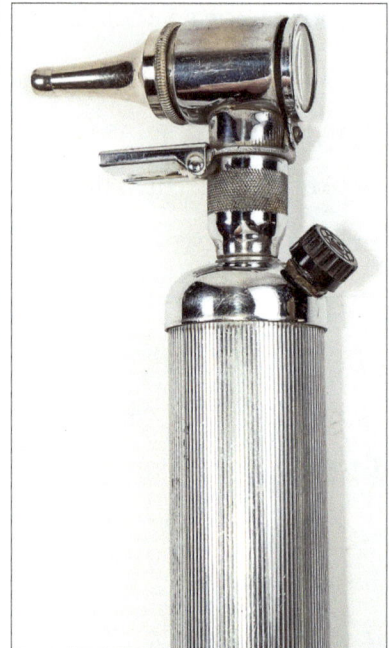

Welch-Allyn otoscope with teaching observation tube (circa 1960s). (Right) Otoscope with unusual rheostat (circa 1910).

usual location, the lamp is positioned in the base of the instrument and its light is transmitted from there to a point in the viewing passage through the instrument by a bundle of optical fibers. The fiber bundle minimizes viewing passage obstruction and assists in providing the uniform, diffuse illumination that is desired without light loss."[133]

A Welch Allyn otoscope in the Touma collection exemplifies the fiber optic illumination technique. It also has an attachment that functions as a pneumatic otoscope, but of more interest is a glass window in the lateral side of the instrument head. The window is situated over a one-way plane mirror that is positioned

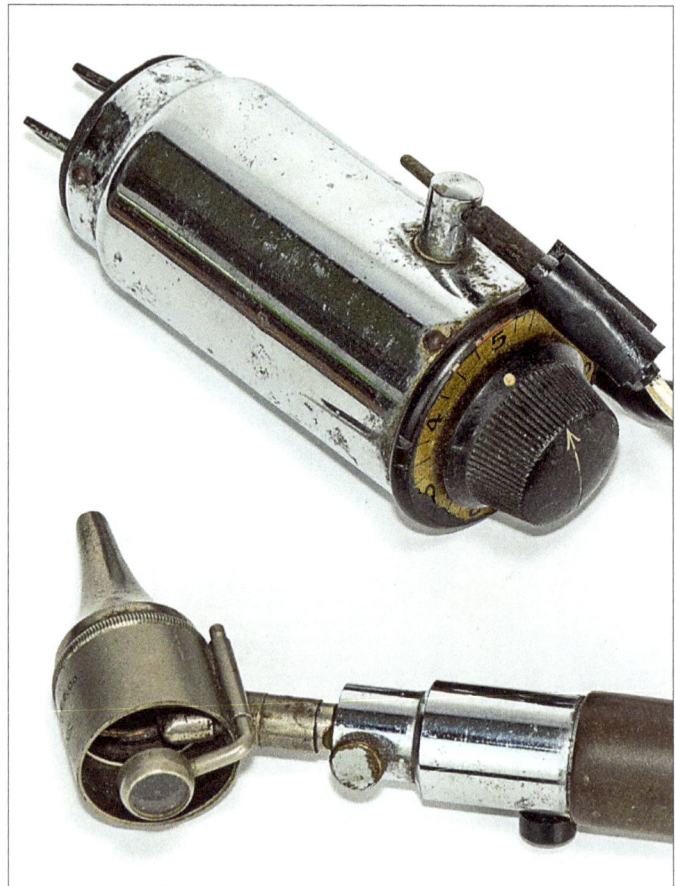

Wappler otoscope, patented in 1910, with early rheostat.

45° to the long axis of the cylinder. Thus, this instrument head, based on concepts developed by 19th-century otologists, can function as a diagnostic and demonstration otoscope.

Controlling the intensity of the light was addressed in the early 19th century. Cameron used a large table top rheostat, while Wappler had a patent in 1910 for a much smaller one. Later they became part of the otoscope, first a rotating knob on the side of the handle. Later it gradually was incorporated with the top of the otoscope handle.

Gowllands, England, otoscope with plastic rheostat.

Early Cameron otoscope with a large tabletop light source and rheostat.

ALIGNMENT OF VISION AND THE LIGHT BEAM

The next challenge was to get the brightest illumination of the tympanic membrane without interfering with the examiner's line of vision. Miller produced an otoscope with the ability to move the light bulb up and down to obtain the brightest lighting.

A similar feature shared by many Cameron otoscopes is a handle with an adjustable light bulb that can be moved in and out of the line of sight. This capability was patented in 1931, and William J. Cameron mentioned it again in his claim for the telescope. Cameron proposed that the light could be positioned to direct the beam precisely at the far opening of the speculum or, if instruments were to be introduced, could be lowered enough to give

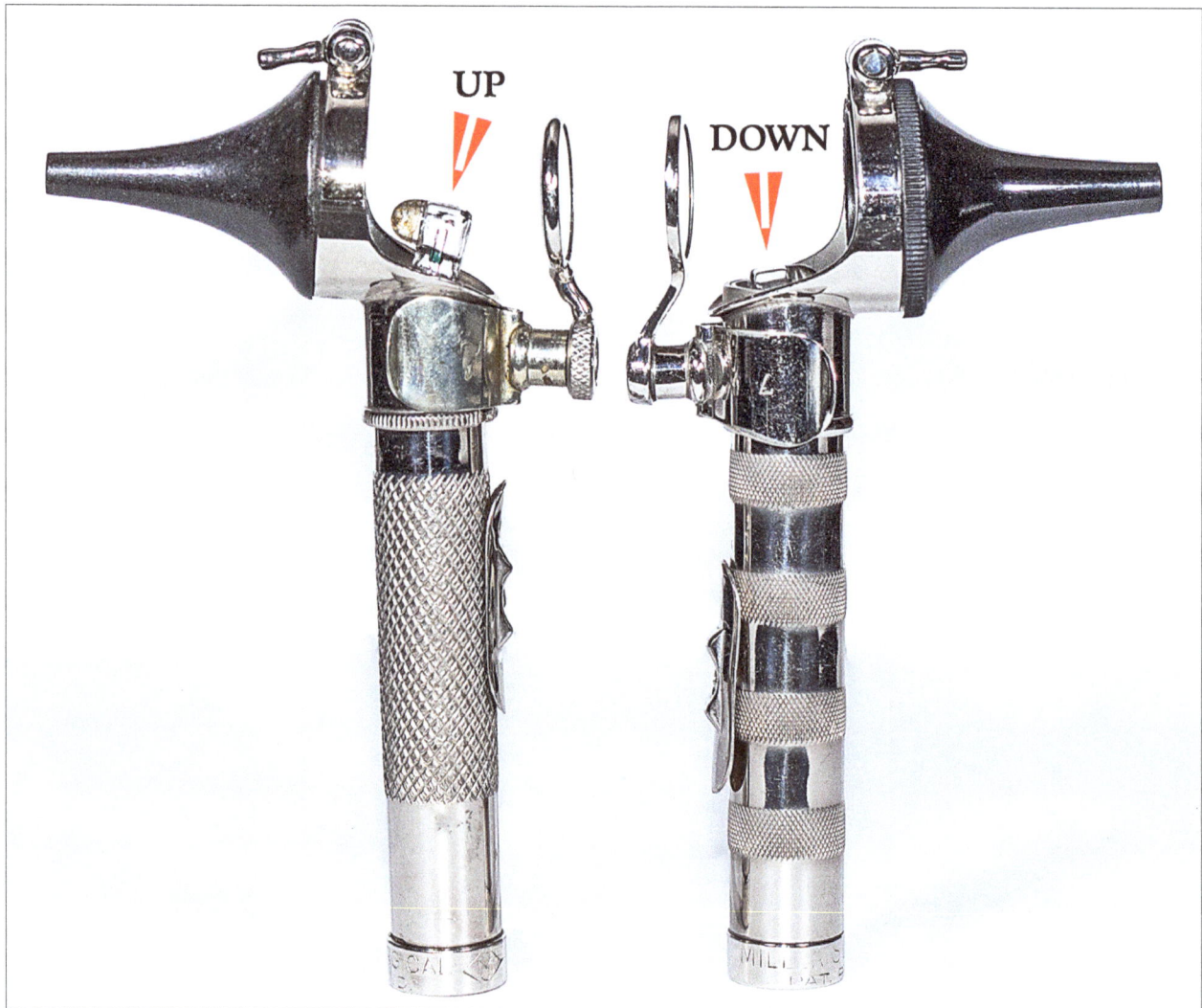

Two Miller otoscopes with a moving light source to maximize the amount of light reaching the eardrum. On the left, the light source is in the up position. On the right, in the down position.

space for operation but still allow satisfactory illumination at the speculum's end.[129] Trying to shine light through to the tip of the otoscope would be an ongoing design challenge during the mid-20th century. As long as the lamp was positioned between the physician's eyes and the tip of the speculum, inventors would need to rely on smaller illumination devices.

By the 1920s and '30s, otoscope makers, especially The National Electric Instrument Company produced many early operating otoscopes. Examples from the Touma collection have a small incandescent bulb positioned in the middle of the instrument head. On one end is a metal ring that holds the plastic ear speculum. This ring sits on a stage that can be moved from side to side to align the line of vision with the light beam. On the other side of the otoscope is a small magnifying lens that the physician can look through. A small plastic hood with a convex lens can then be placed over the bulb to both eliminate excess glare and concentrate the light toward the patient's ear. A disadvantage of this mechanism is that the trajectory of the light beam is not directly parallel with the user's line of sight.

National Electric addressed this misalignment with a device called the Shadowless Central Aperture Specialists' Otoscope. As the name suggests, it relies on a centrally perforated mirror that redirects a beam of light toward

the speculum tip without obstructing the physician's view. A magnifying lens at the back of the instrument head functions as the eyepiece. With both the Simple and Specialists' models, the stage on which the speculum ring sits can be adjusted left and right in a plane orthogonal to the line of sight. While this rectilinear adjustment facilitated instrumentation, adjustment was needed to throw the light toward the tip of the speculum.

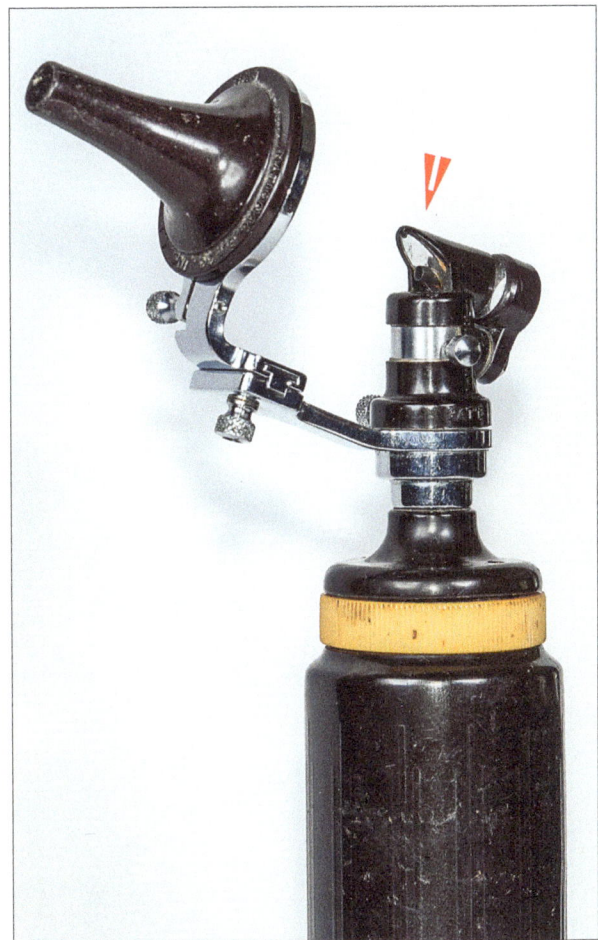

National Electric "shadowless central aperture specialists' otoscope" with a 45-degree mirror, marked by an arrow, to reflect and direct the light to the center of the speculum.

Two National otoscopes with horizontal movement of the ear speculum to direct the light beam to the center of the ear speculum.

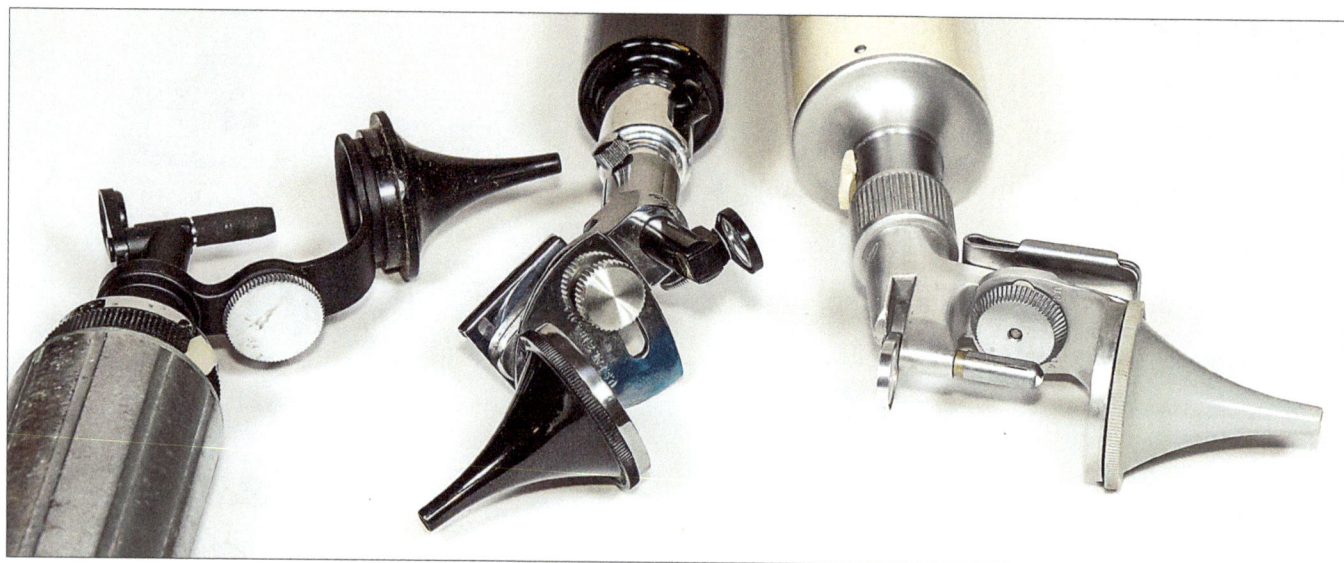

Three otoscopes with an accurate movement of the speculum stage to bring the light beam on the center of the speculum. (Left) National otoscope. (Middle and right) Bausch & Lomb otoscopes.

American Optical developed the "Ful-Vue" otoscope. The light source moves in an accurate path relative to the speculum so that the light remains trained to the depth of the speculum. Immediately above the light source is a magnifying lens to provide a better view of the eardrum.

Bausch & Lomb's "Arc-Vue," patented in 1939, is a great example of this effort in otoscope illumination, with a design found primarily on Bausch & Lomb operating otoscopes made from the 1940s to 1960s. The idea behind the Arc-Vue is that the connection between the stage on which the speculum holder sits and the rest of the device, including the light source and magnification lens, hinges at an arcuate slot in the speculum stage. This allows the larger opening of the speculum to move right and left

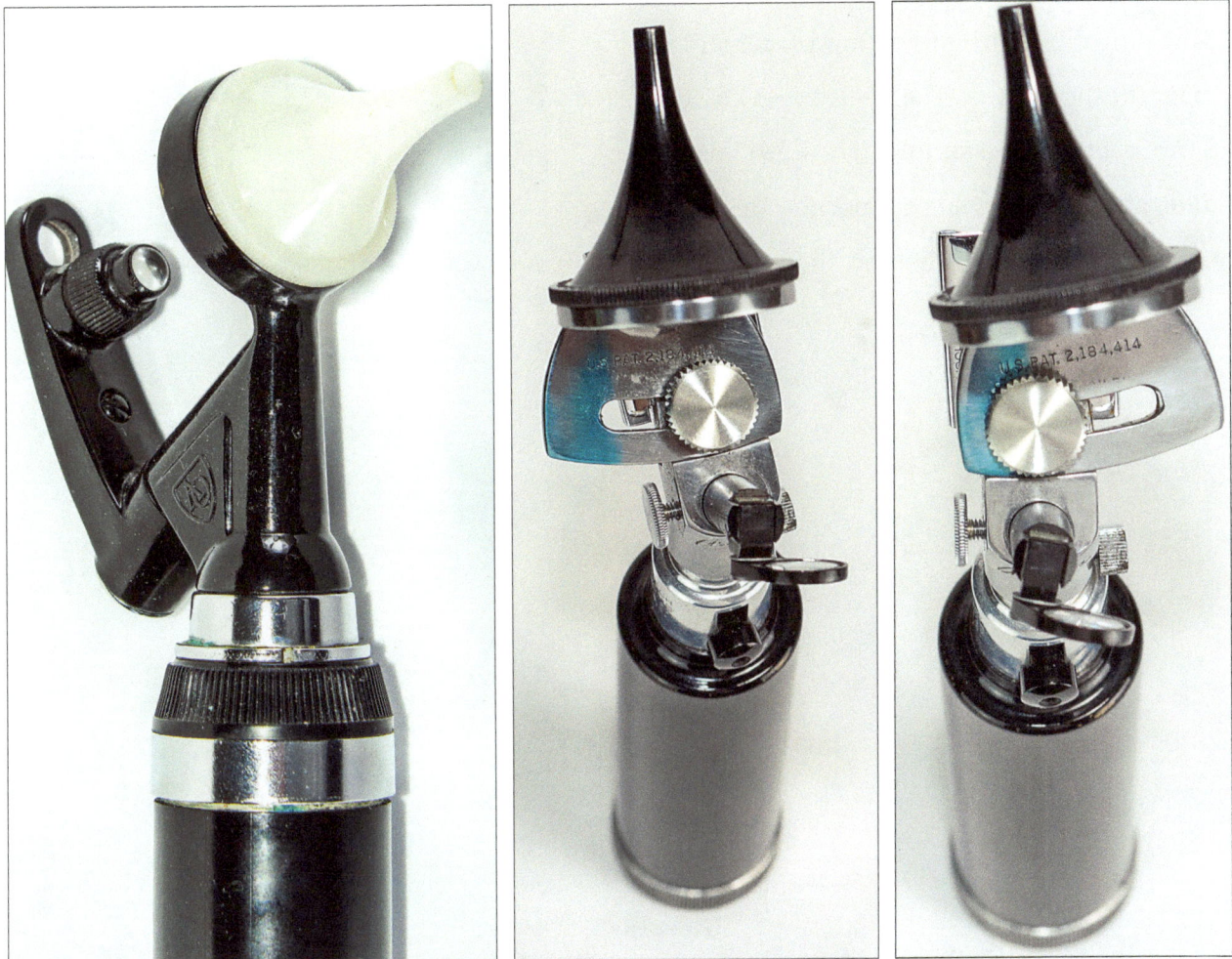

(Left) Ful-Vue otoscope by American Optical (circa 1940s). The light source moves in an arcuate path relative to the speculum in order for the light to remain trained on the tip of the speculum. (Middle-Right) Bausch & Lomb Arc-Vue otoscope (circa 1930). The movement of the stage ensures that the light remains focused on the tip of the speculum.

in an arc, with the tip of the speculum remaining stationary relative to the lines of sight and light. Thus, the light beam is always trained on the tip of the speculum to illuminate the field of inspection or operation. This allows the physician to maneuver the nearer opening of the speculum to more easily introduce instruments without disrupting the transmission of light.[130]

MAGNIFICATION

Several examples from the Touma Medical Museum illustrate interesting placement of magnification lenses. The Wellsworth DeZeng Simplex otoscope, stamped with a 1915 patent date, attempts to create a binocular device by placing two eyeholes behind the instrument

Wellsworth DeZeng with binocular lens (patent December 21, 1915).

Early "binocular" otoscopes. (Left) Allen & Hanberrys Ltd. otoscope, (middle) Bausch & Lomb otoscope, and (right) Wellsworth DeZeng patented December 21, 1915.

head, each housing magnification lenses which are fixed in place, so instrumentation cannot be accommodated. This device's illumination technique — an incandescent bulb extending from the handle and covered by a hood in the instrument head — is an additional limitation, as there is neither a means by which light is concentrated nor any directing mechanism. Its date suggests that the Wellsworth design was behind the times, since more sophisticated illumination techniques, as evidenced in the Wappler design, were available as early as 1910. The Wellsworth brand name was associated with all American Optical Company products from 1916 until 1927, when it was reportedly dropped because it became more familiar in the marketplace than the name of the manufacturer itself.

The second example is more similar to the split magnification lens otoscope made by Allen and Hanbury's Limited, a former British pharmaceutical company that also made surgical instruments. It had a magnification lens on a rotary dial affixed to the back of the instrument head. This lens was positioned 180° from an open hole with no lens.

The examiner could both obtain a magnified view of the tympanic membrane through one opening and introduce an instrument through the other opening.

In 1931, inventor William J. Cameron, founder of Cameron Surgical Specialty Company in Chicago, applied for a patent for a device he called the illuminated telescope for instruments:

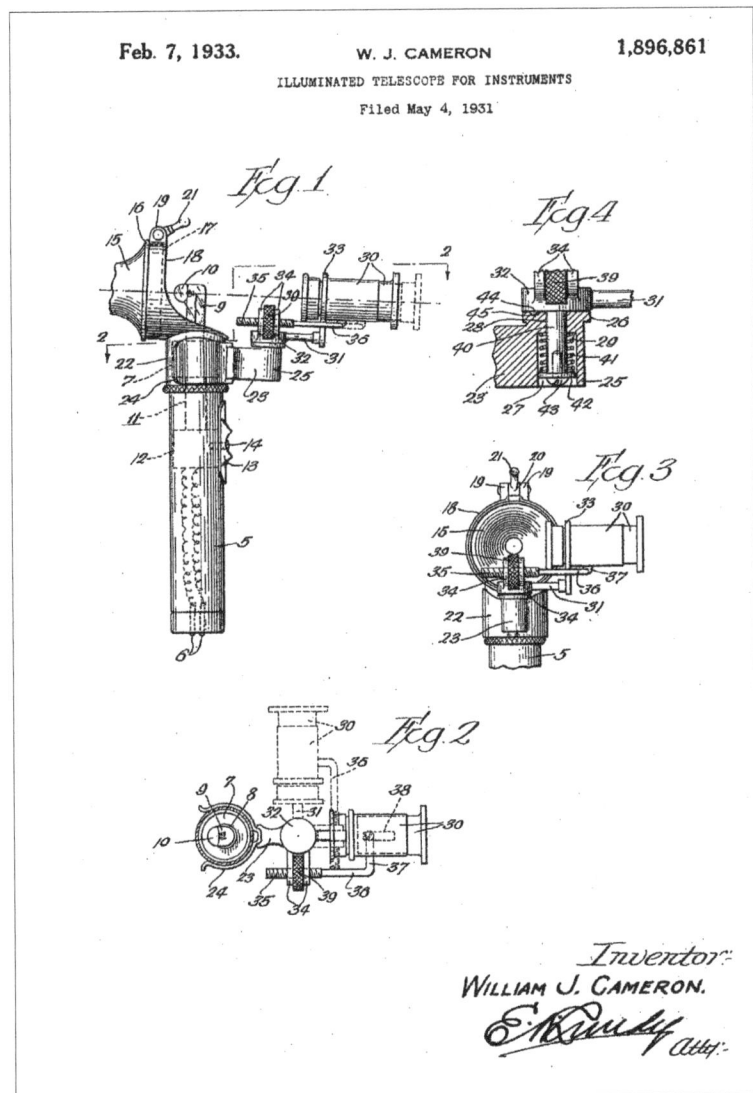

Patent application for W.J. Cameron's "Illuminated Telescope for Instruments," May 4, 1931.

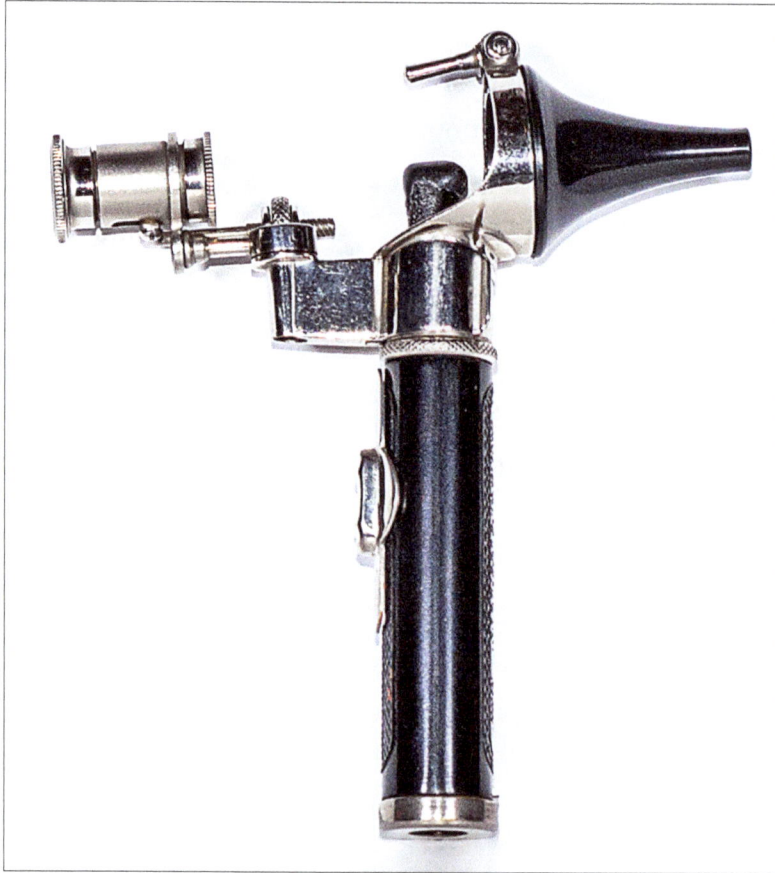

Cameron "telescope" otoscope, patent #1-896-861, May 4, 1931.

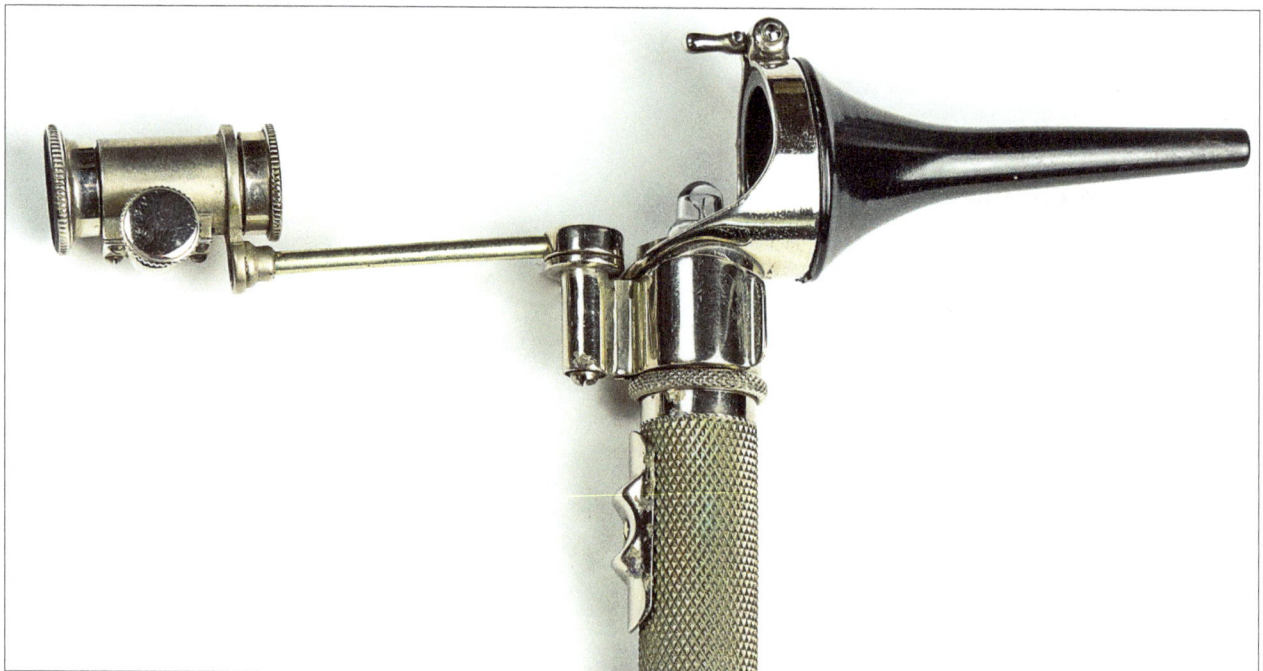

Telescopic otoscope by Cameron Surgical Specialty Co., Chicago (circa 1925).

"The viewing device comprises a pair of telescopically arranged tubes, carrying the usual lenses for magnification, which tubes are adapted to be moved relative to each other for the purpose of focusing the lenses upon the area illuminated by the lamp. The telescope is mounted on the bracket so that it may be swung laterally, so that it will be out of the way when the surgeon is using instruments in the speculum."[127]

Cameron's telescope was officially patented in 1933, but a simple magnification lens would ultimately win out as the preferred means of magnification for otoscopes.

Gowllands Ltd. developed an operating microscope with a binocular lens and Deleau speculum; Bausch & Lomb, on the other hand, followed the new trend and developed its own binocular otoscope.

W.J. Cameron's telescope had an approximately one-inch-long complex lens system to provide a much larger image of the tympanic membrane. Later, Cameron developed a telescopic otoscope with a similar lens system; however, it sat about two inches farther away from the ear speculum.

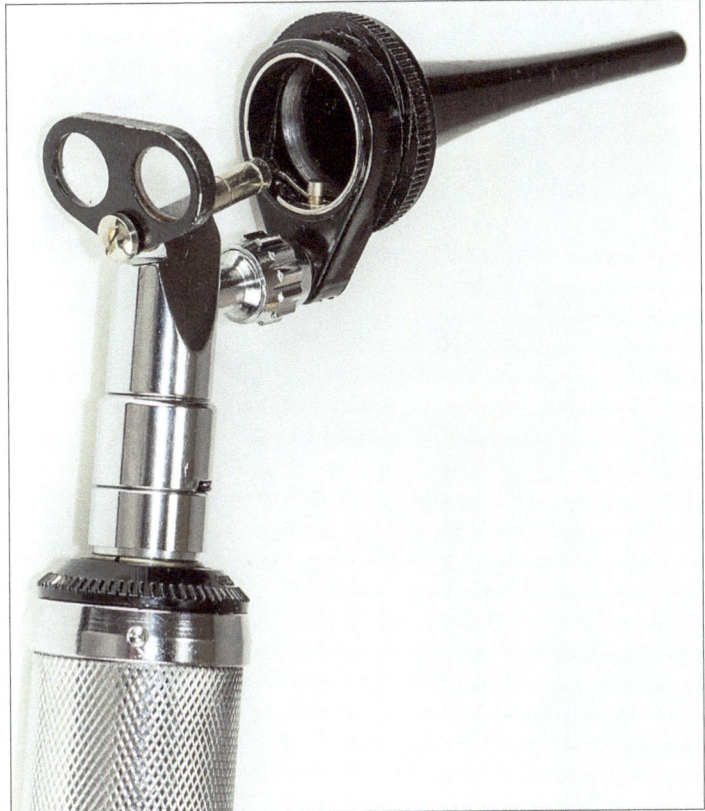

Gowllands otoscope, England, with binocular lens and Deleau speculum.

Early Keeler otoscope with complex magnifying system.

(Left) Keeler diagnostic and (Middle) Keeler operating otoscopes with complex magnifying lens and focus adjustment. (Right) Keeler otoscope with stationary single magnifying lens and pneumatic otoscopy cannula.

Other examples of the complex lens system in the Touma collection include an early Keeler otoscope and other versions of operating and diagnostic Keeler otoscopes with more advanced magnifying systems with better focusing mechanism.

Most of the otoscopes had a single magnifying lens, however several otoscopes have a second lens to improve the magnification of the tympanic membrane. In addition they increase the versatility of the otoscope to be used as a diagnostic or operative purpose by removing or adding the front lens.

Solving lighting, magnification, and other challenges did not stop inventors from further improving and modifying the otoscope. The Touma collection has several otoscopes with special features, such as the Miller otoscope with an angled handle. It is similar to a regular otoscope, but, for no specific reason, the handle is angled. An unmarked otoscope in the collection has ear specula and other attachments that

(Left) Miller otoscope with angled handle. (Top) Unmarked otoscope with one of several attachments in place.

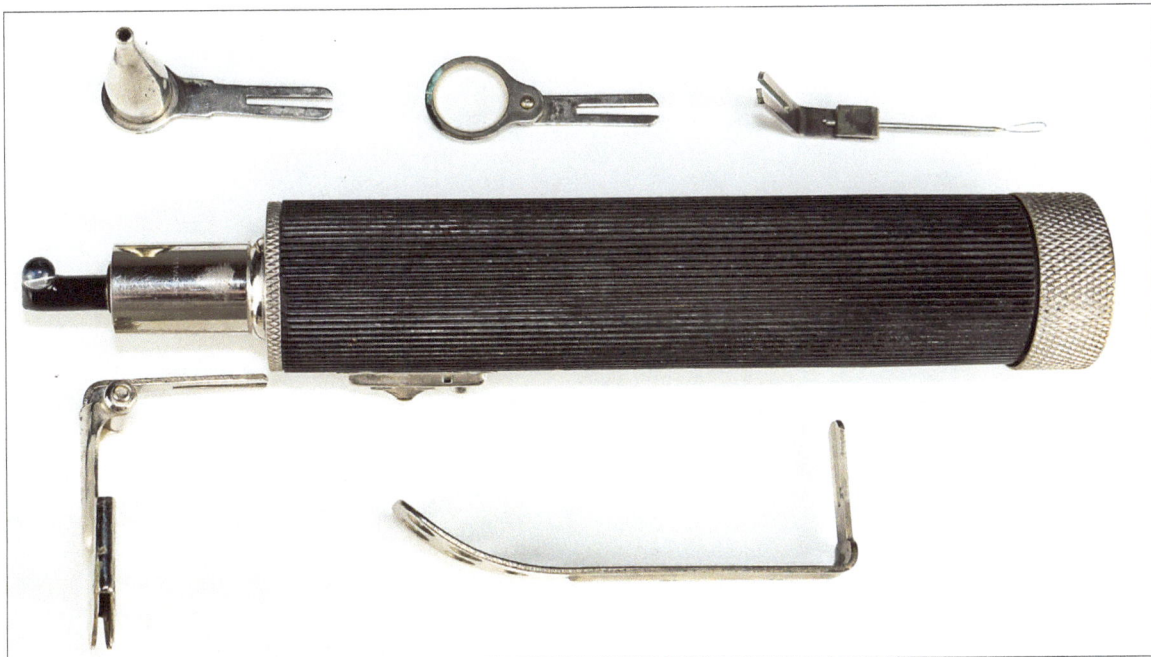

Unmarked otoscope with multiple attachments that can be inserted into the body of the otoscope.

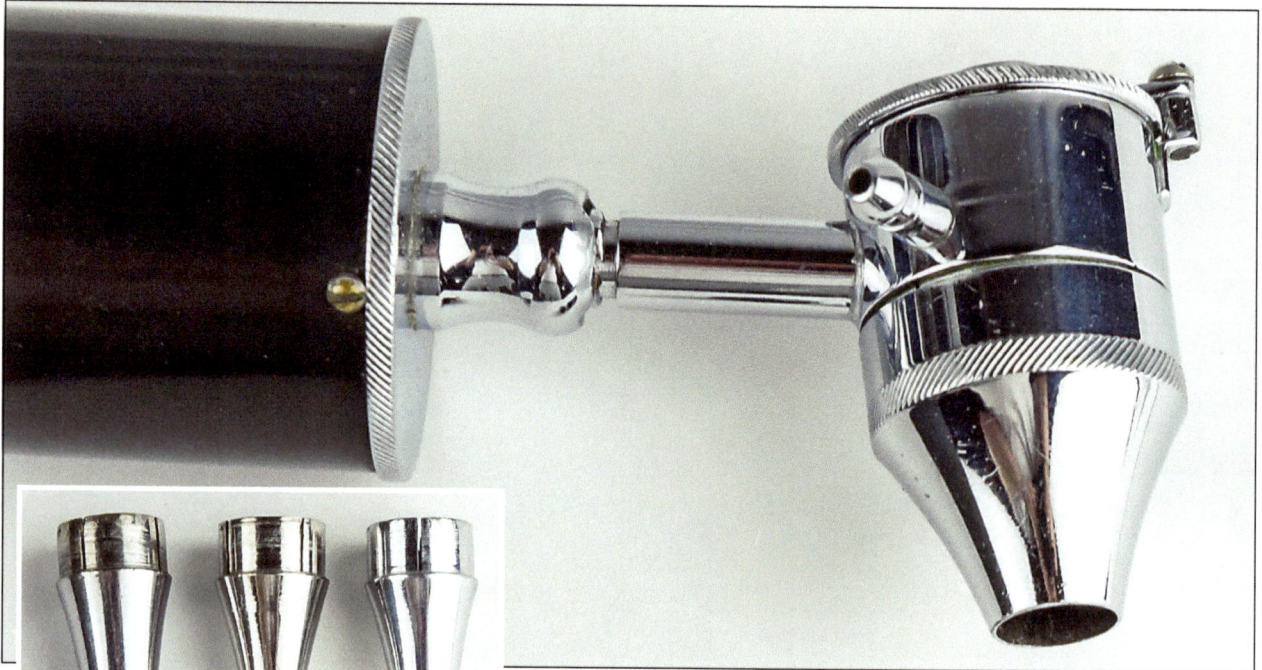

Houston pediatric otoscope with three small specula.
Label reads: "Huston Bros Co. surgical supplies,
established 1887 Chicago."

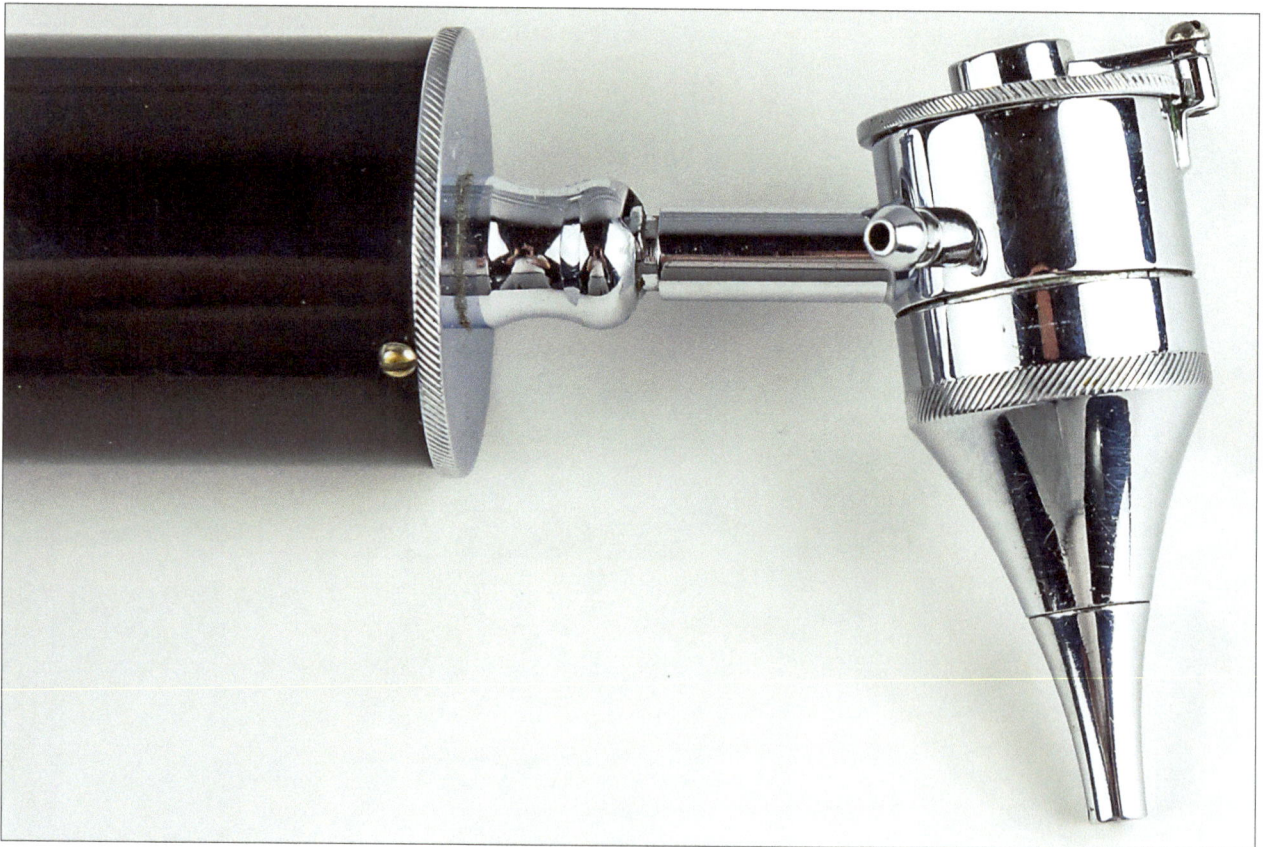

Houston pediatric otoscope with speculum in place.

can be inserted into the handle of the otoscope; a light bulb sits directly on top of the body of the otoscope. Another interesting otoscope is the American Optical Company otoscope with a plugged-in speculum. The difference between it and the previous otoscope is that the magnifying lens is part of the body, whereas with the previous otoscope the lens had to be inserted into the body. General Optical Company produced a diagnostic otoscope with a closed chamber; its unique feature is that slits on the ends of both specula allow instruments to be introduced from outside the speculum.

Theodore Hamblin Ltd. Dispensing Opticians, London W1 and Provinces, produced an otoscope with an off-center stem connecting the battery-contained body to the scope itself. Another unusual instrument is the Burgess otoscope, made in the U.S. in the 1930s, with a long stem between the battery-contained body and the scope. The area housing the light bulb sits on an angle, making it difficult to align the line of vision and the light beam. Houston Bros Co. Surgical Supplies, established in 1887 in Chicago, Illinois, produced a pediatric otoscope, with three small specula that could be inserted into the opening of the short stationary speculum.

Theodore Hamblin Ltd. otoscope with an off-center stem.

In the 1920s and early 1930s, several manufacturers, including Boehm, Cameron, and Winchester, produced otoscopes with various-sized openings on the edges of the magnifying lenses — from small to half-moon — to allow for instrumentation. Some of these devices had ventilation cannulas, which could be sealed with the physician's thumb for pneumatic otoscopy.

California inventor John Hotchkiss claimed that fiber optic light did not adequately address the parallax between the lines of sight and light. Like so many inventors before him, Hotchkiss set out to make a device that would solve this longstanding problem. His otoscope, patented in 1971, seems to step back in time, however,

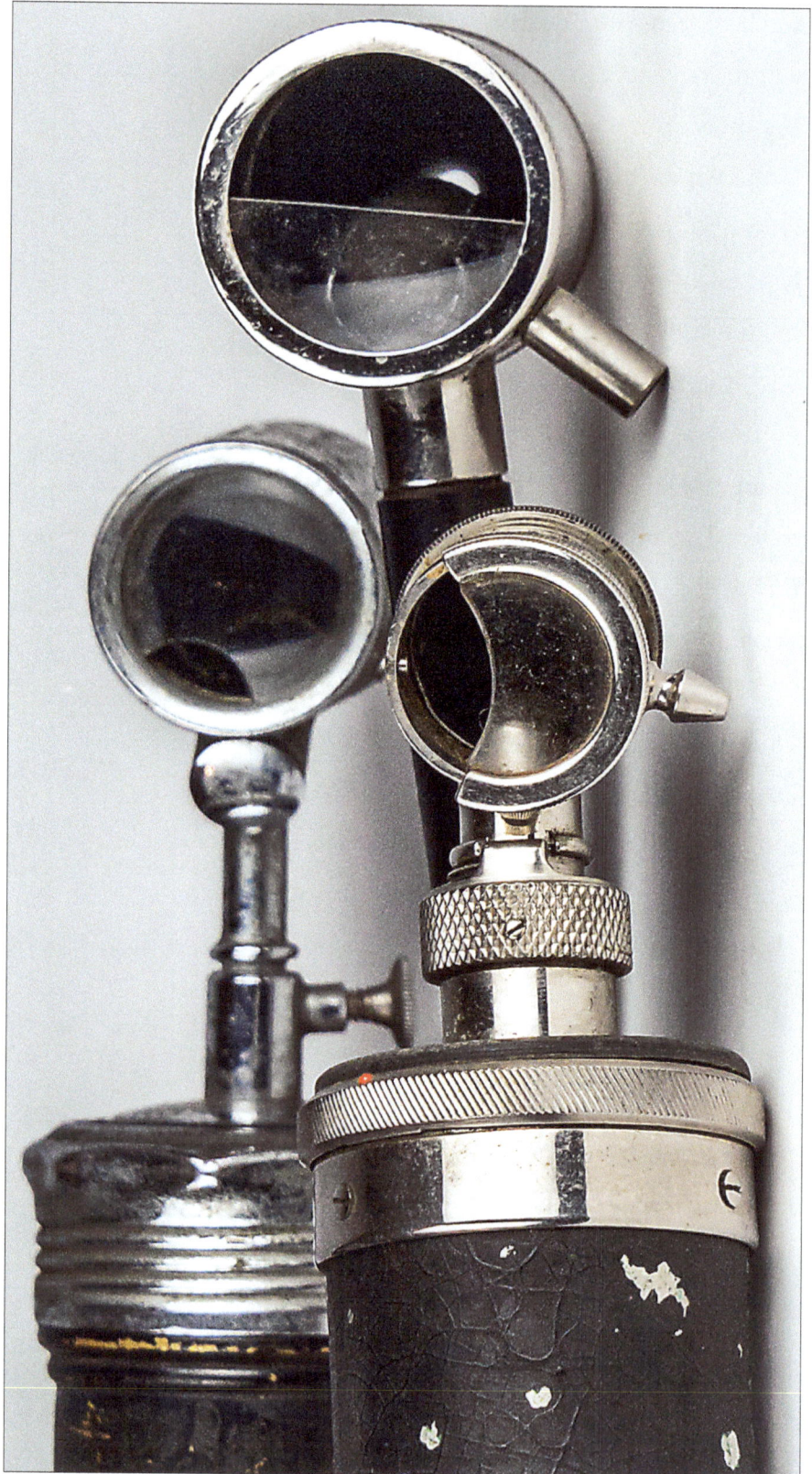

Three operating otoscopes with varios lensa openings for instrumentation. (Left) Boehm otoscope - circa 1930s, (Middle) Cameron otoscope and (Right) Winchester otoscope - circa 1920s.

by relying on reflected light from an incandescent bulb for illumination. The reflector then redirects the light toward a biconvex lens such that the light is concentrated as it travels toward the tympanic membrane. An interesting point about the Hotchkiss otoscope is the method of pneumoscopy it employs. The end of the instrument head has an opening that can be occluded by the examiner's thumb to provide a seal.[134]

The Hotchkiss otoscope illustrates the challenges that can underlie what appears to be a simple task. Although it is still available today, its illumination mechanism and revisiting of Brunton's principles, was not widely embraced. Instead, fiber optic devices that provided direct illumination would prevail in diagnostic and operative otoscopy.

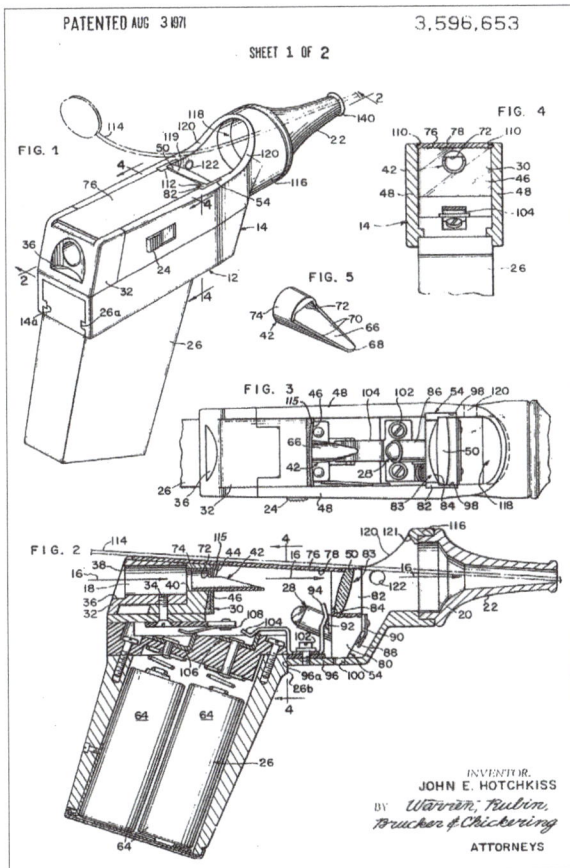

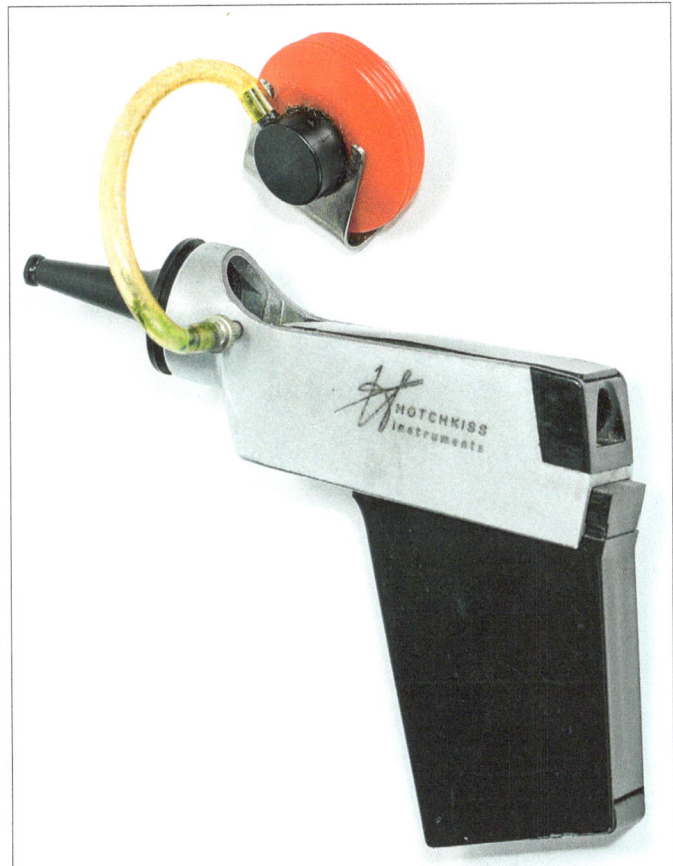

(Left) Patent application for John Hotchkiss' "Otoscope," August 3, 1971. (Right) The Hotchkiss otoscope 1971.

PNEUMATIC OTOSCOPES

A year before Brunton's otoscope appeared in the *Lancet*, German physician Emil Siegle introduced the first pneumatic otoscope, which served as the basis for pneumatic designs to follow. Key-Aberg writes, "[Siegle's] original model has long since been abandoned and replaced by a number of other funnel types, constructed according to the same principle. … Most pneumatic ear specula consist, firstly, of a metal cylinder attached to a small rubber balloon, within which cylinder there is arranged a magnifying lens, and secondly, of an adjustable metal funnel, which can be affixed hermetically to the cylinder in question, and which is of a width corresponding approximately in every instance to the auricular tube's lumen."[86]

Siegle's initial pneumatic otoscope had a rubber hose with a mouthpiece and a speculum

Siegle pneumatic otoscope with rubber bulb, manufactured by Sklar, U.S.

made of hard, black rubber, similar to Politzer's.[87] Later he replaced the mouthpiece with a rubber bulb.

In 1873, Voltolini modified the Brunton design by making it airtight and adding a rubber tube attachment, thereby creating a pneumatic otoscope.[88] While it was an interesting modification of two celebrated designs, Voltolini's device had two flaws that were also inherent in Siegle's original design. First, the speculum used by Siegle and Voltolini did not ensure a proper seal with the external ear canal, thereby limiting the tympanic membrane's response to air compression and rarefaction. This shortcoming could be overcome by placing a perforated rubber cork into the canal through which the speculum could pass, forming a proper seal.[89] Second, when examiners provided changes in pressure by mouth, some amount of water would inevitably condense within the metal chamber and on the lens, obstructing their view of the patient's tympanic membrane. This could be addressed by using a hand-operated rubber bulb.[90] A syringe could also be used to alter pressure within the system.[91]

Eysell addressed this shortcoming in Siegle's design in 1872 with his own pneumatic otoscope. The speculum Eysell used had a cap-like

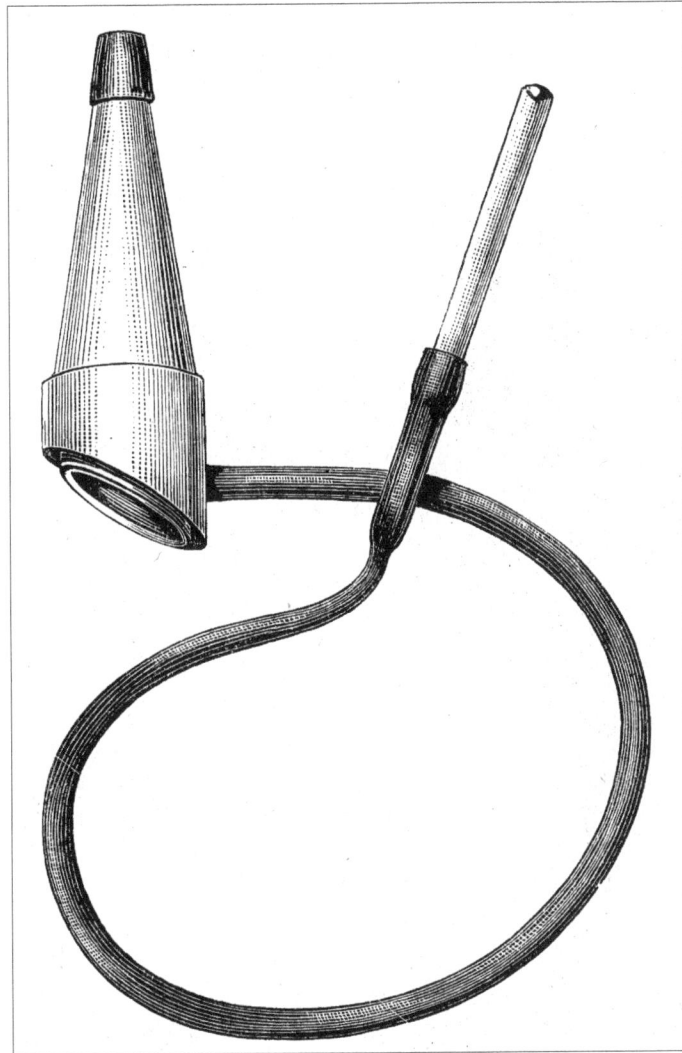

Eysell pneumatic otoscope. The rubber hose is connected to a mouth piece, allowing the physician to provide pressure change for insufflation and rarefaction.

expansion on the end that would be placed in the ear canal, presumably to provide more consistent seals between the device and the canal.[92] Eysell, who served as Schwartze's assistant, also made many contributions to the field in his own right, including a worthy description of the annular ligament.[93]

Burnett's initial modification of Siegle's otoscope was essentially the same as Eysell's:

"This is practically a metallic Gruber speculum transformed into a Siegle pneumatic speculum, or otoscope, by the addition of a glass lid. Its extreme length is five and one-half centimeters, and its diameters at its metal end are six millimetres vertically and four millimetres horizontally. This renders it more adaptable to the shape of the meatus," he writes in *A Text-book on Diseases of the Ear, Nose and Throat*.[94]

Burnett also advocated the use of a syringe for compression and rarefaction in pneumatic otoscopes. Into the early 1900s, this manual method was seen by some, including Professor Francis Packard of the Philadelphia Polyclinic, as superior to the electric-powered devices that would follow.[95]

Belgian otologist Charles Delstanche developed his own syringe-like rarefacteur. Depressing the piston in this device would engage a spring so that when the piston was

Early Delstanche pneumatic otoscope with metal air pump.

released it would return the device to a preset volume. This could be used by the patient for therapeutic massage of the tympanic membrane and was widely promoted for such use.[96] Delstanche's rarefacteur was also used by many as an attachment to the Siegle otoscope to provide predictable changes in pressure.[97] Founder of the Belgian Society of Otology, Laryngology, and Rhinology, Delstanche was a famed otologist in his own right. A friend to Politzer, Delstanche studied and excelled in some of otology's European capitals, such as Bologna and London.[98]

Many in the early 1900s maintained that hand-operated pneumatic otoscopes were superior to electric models. Nevertheless, it was inevitable that the latter would eventually gain some foothold in the field. One of the earliest examples of this is the Breitung pump, which could be used with any compatible speculum, including a Siegle, as noted in James Love's *Diseases of the Ear*:

"The most efficient method of applying this pneumo-massage is by Breitung's pump. This pump should be attached to a small motor connected with the main, or to a battery the voltage of which suits the motor. The speed at which the pump moves is regulated by the introduction of suitable resistances, and the effect of the stroke on the structures within the middle ear may be regulated by making the fitting placed in the external auditory canal more or less tight. ... The effect is watched by the surgeon through a Siegle's speculum, which is placed in the canal and connected by a rubber tube with the pump."[99]

While the Breitung pump certainly offered advantages, this arrangement with the Siegle speculum represented no real advancement in the design of the pneumatic otoscope. However, progress was noted as early as 1912 in a text by W. Franklin Coleman, former president of and professor of ophthalmology at the Medical School of Chicago. The pneumatic otoscope Coleman described is more familiar in construction and represents an early example of the modern design.[100] He mentioned the use of ear pumps in conjunction with a pneumatic otoscope. Whether he meant an electric device like the Breitung pump or a simple handheld rubber bulb is unclear. Nonetheless, simplicity would eventually win out and the rubber bulb would remain the more widely used mode of operating a pneumatic otoscope. In actuality, the more popular use for electric ear pumps was derived from their therapeutic effect with pneumo-massage, which Politzer describes as "especially applicable in adhesive processes of the middle ear and in otosclerosis."[101]

Electric pumps provided an exciting way for physicians to investigate the tension of the eardrum, but the greatest benefit electricity offered pneumatic otoscopy came in the wide range of light sources it made available to clinicians. These advancements would be made in regard to otoscopes as inventors began to take the investigative advantage of a pneumatic device into consideration while designing diagnostic otoscopes.

In contrast to the purely operative otoscope is the diagnostic otoscope. One of the earliest examples in the Touma collection is a wall-powered otoscope made by Cameron Surgical Specialty Company. The light source is a small bulb with a convex lens like the Wappler device, and an eyepiece with a magnifying lens screws into the back. A speculum can then be affixed to the front of the otoscope and a rubber hose can be inserted into a hole in the main body of the otoscope to make a pneumatic device.

A battery-powered diagnostic Welch Allyn otoscope dated to 1924 also uses a small light bulb with a convex lens for direct illumination. It, too, has a pneumatic option, but the magnifying lens is on a swinging arm and the eyepiece is a glass window that can be screwed on and off the rear of the instrument head. Presumably, this eyepiece could be removed to allow for instrumentation and the magnifying lens brought into view, but the space allowed for operation with this otoscope does not compare favorably with the amount available with National Electric's devices.

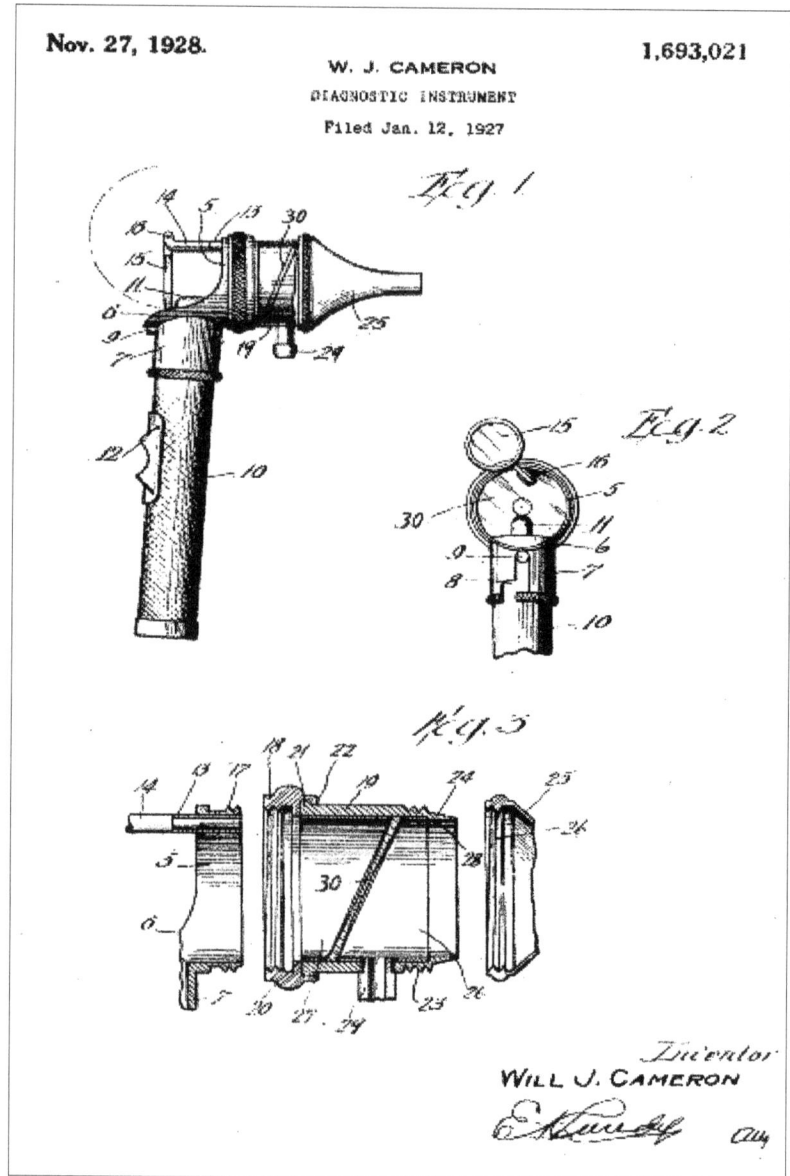

Patent application for W.J. Cameron's "Diagnostic Instrument," November 12, 1927.

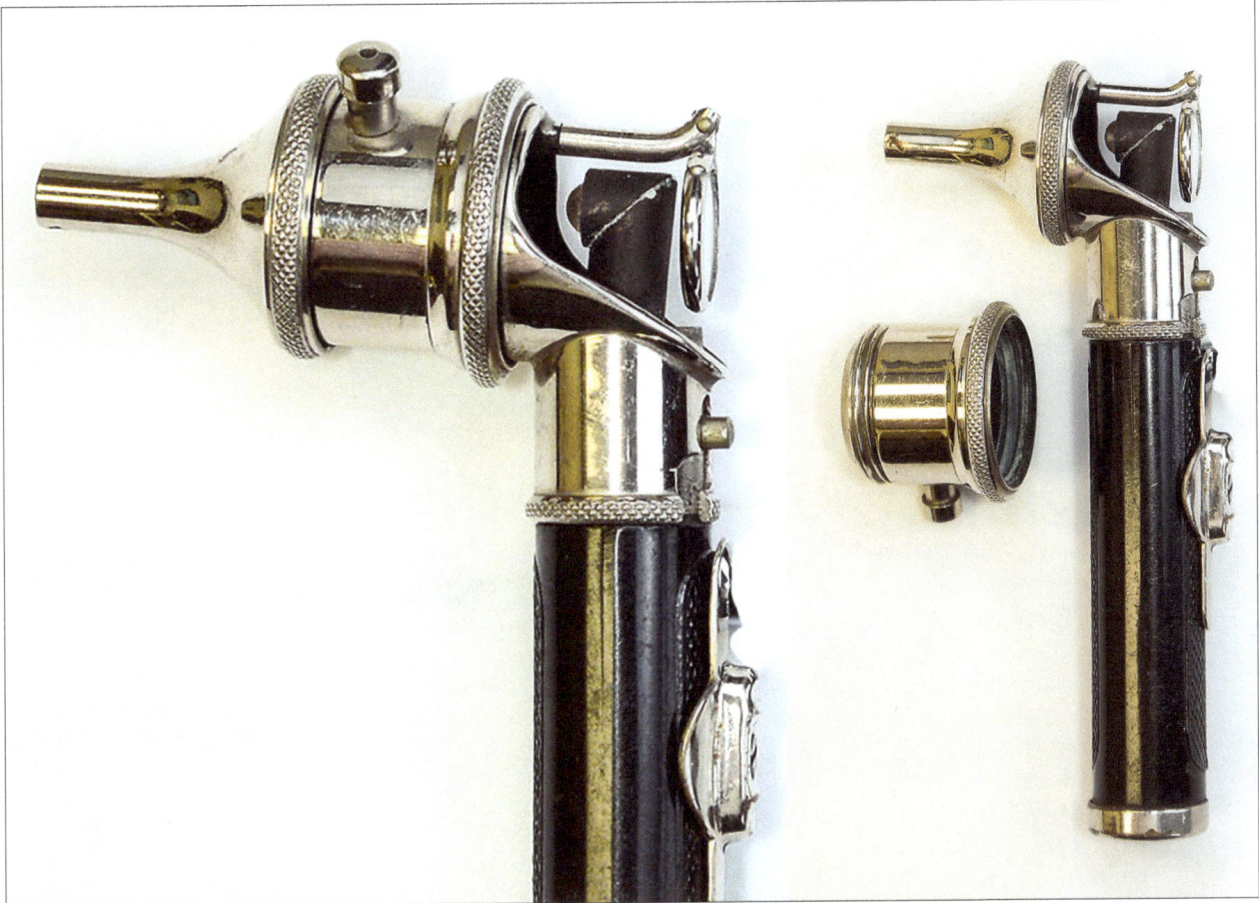

Cameron operating otoscope (November 12, 1927). The pneumatic chamber can be removed, turning it into an operating otoscope.

Welch Allyn otoscope (circa 1930s). On the left, the lens is screwed in place, creating an airtight space for pneumatic otoscopy. On the right, the lens is unscrewed and opened to enable the introduction of instruments.

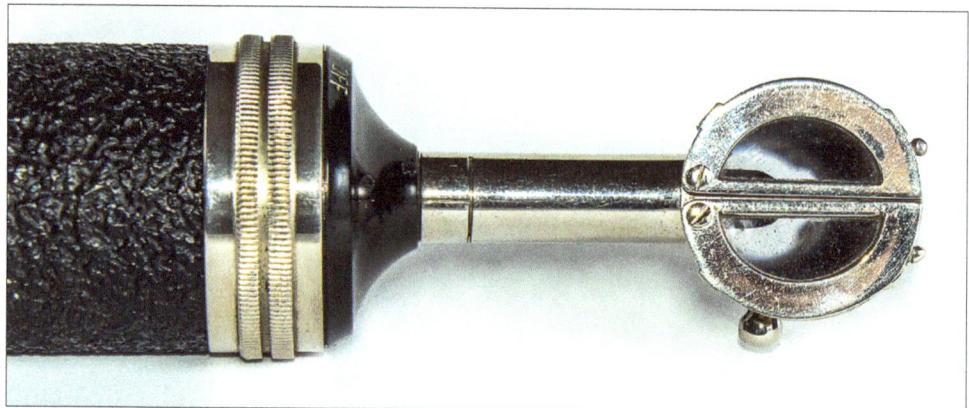

General Optical half-moon-lens otoscope allowed for dual diagnostic and operative otoscope (circa 1920s).

Dedicated operative and diagnostic otoscopes allowed manufacturers to design instruments specifically for one purpose. However, the utility of a device that could be used in both pursuits was undoubtedly appealing to physicians. An otoscope made by the General Optical Company provides an example. It features two half-moon magnifying lenses that can be brought together to produce a solitary eyepiece that creates a sealed fit. Within the body of the instrument is a small bulb with a convex lens for direct illumination and ear speculum opposite the eyepiece. With the two magnifying lenses brought to a close, the device could be used as a pneumatic otoscope. When the physician needed to operate, one of the halves could be opened to accommodate instrumentation while retaining a magnified view of the tympanic membrane. Interestingly, the speculum associated with this device has two slits at its narrow end, presumably to permit maneuvering of instruments.

A 1939 Wappler otoscope achieves the same two functions with a magnifying lens that screws into place to provide a seal and a smaller magnifying lens that can be brought into view once the larger eyepiece is removed and the instrument head is opened.

In *Modern Otology*, published in 1930, Joseph Keeler describes a similar surgical otoscope that gained popularity for this capability.[126]

In the late 1920s, Keeler produced an otoscope with a magnifying lens that screwed in place to provide a seal, facilitating its use as a pneumatic otoscope. Its prism lighting and smaller lens were useful when used as an operative otoscope.

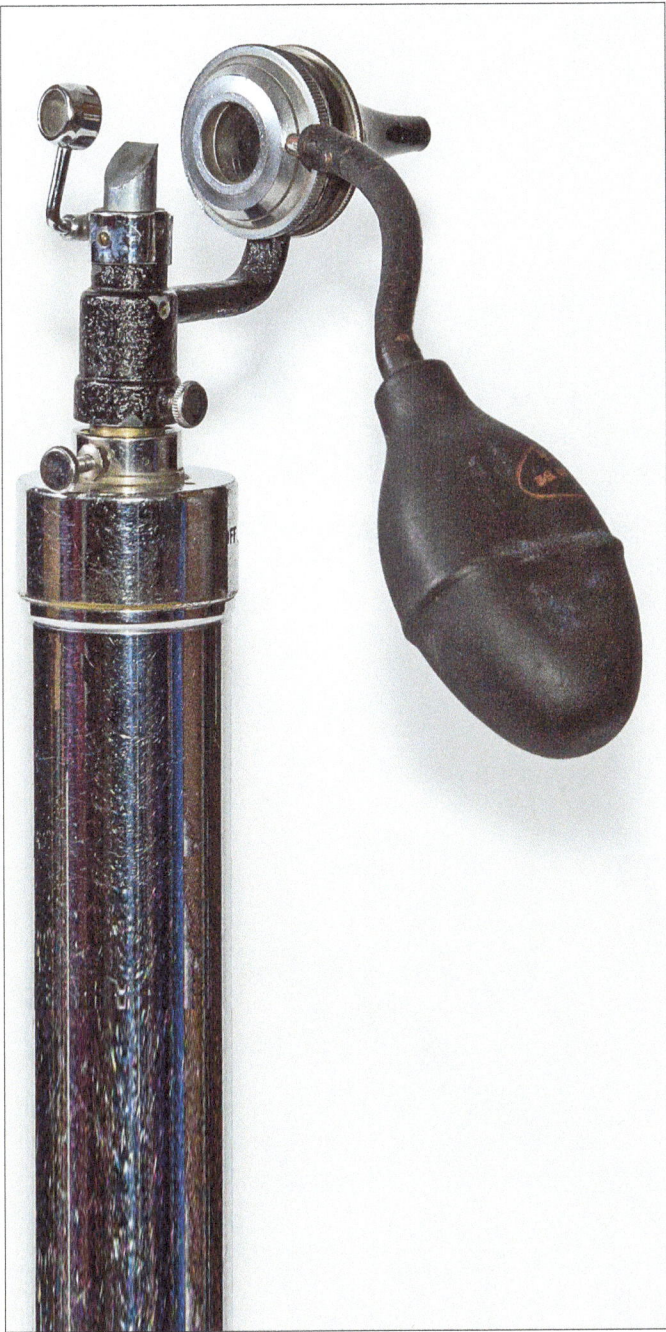

(Left) Early Keeler otoscope (circa 1920s) in pneumatic otoscopy mode. (Right) Keeler otoscope in operating mode, created by removing the magnifying lens.

(Left) Burgess otoscope with attached pneumatic bulb. (Right) Argus otoscope with pneumatic chamber and dual magnification capabilities (circa 1930).

The Touma collection has additional interesting pneumatic otoscopes, such as the "Burgess" otoscope with a long stem connecting the handle to the chamber, an "Argus", strictly pneumatic otoscope with dual lenses, a "Sklar" Siegel otoscope, and a "National" pneumatic otoscope with bulb.

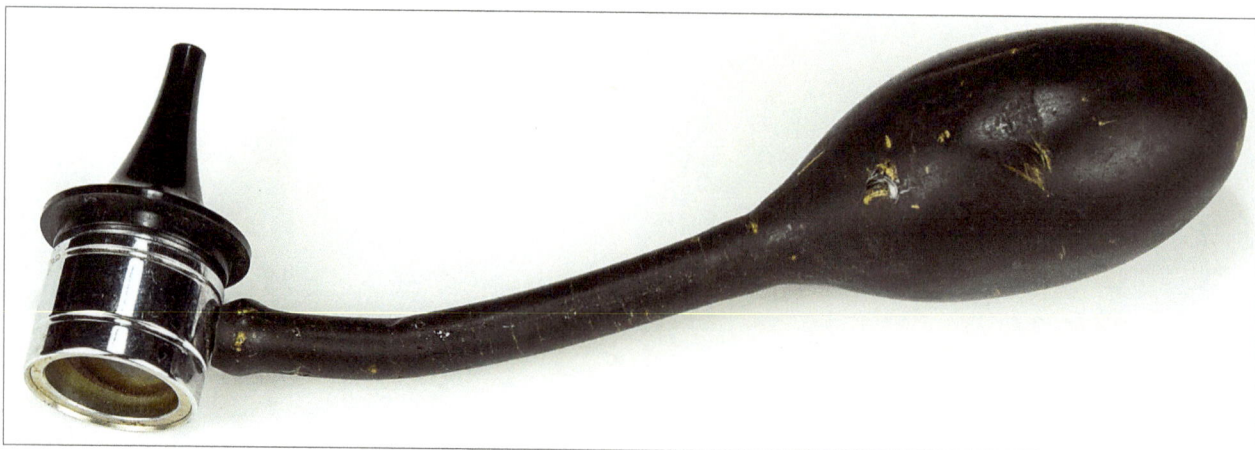

Pneumatic otoscope, National E.I. Co., New York, otoscope set. It has "U S, STOCK NO. 3-540-200" imprinted on the box (circa 1930s).

EAR CLEANING

A patent ear canal is a crucial element in otoscopy; thus, any discussion of the field is incomplete without some attention to preparing the ear canal for examination. Wilde addresses this in one of his textbooks:

"In the previous description of the method of examining the external and middle ear, it has been presumed that the external auditory conduit is free; it may, however, and it often does, happen, that we are unable to explore the passage, or obtain a view of the membrana tympani, owing to obstruction of the former

Ivory syringes (late 18th or early 19th century).

Pewter syringe with wooden plunger (late 18th century).

with cerumen, collections of hair, or thickened and detached epithelium, the muco-purulent secretion consequent upon otorrhea, or foreign bodies of any description; and therefore it is sometimes necessary to have recourse to the operation of syringing merely to assist our diagnosis. Simple as this operation may appear, and frequently as it is resorted to by uneducated persons, it is one which requires some degree of tact, caution, and dexterity, in its performance."[135]

In an otology textbook for medical students published in 1899, Albert H. Buck, professor at the College of Physicians and Surgeons of Columbia University, agrees with Wilde that only properly trained individuals should attempt to clean the ear canal. He suggests first using forceps and curettes to remove debris

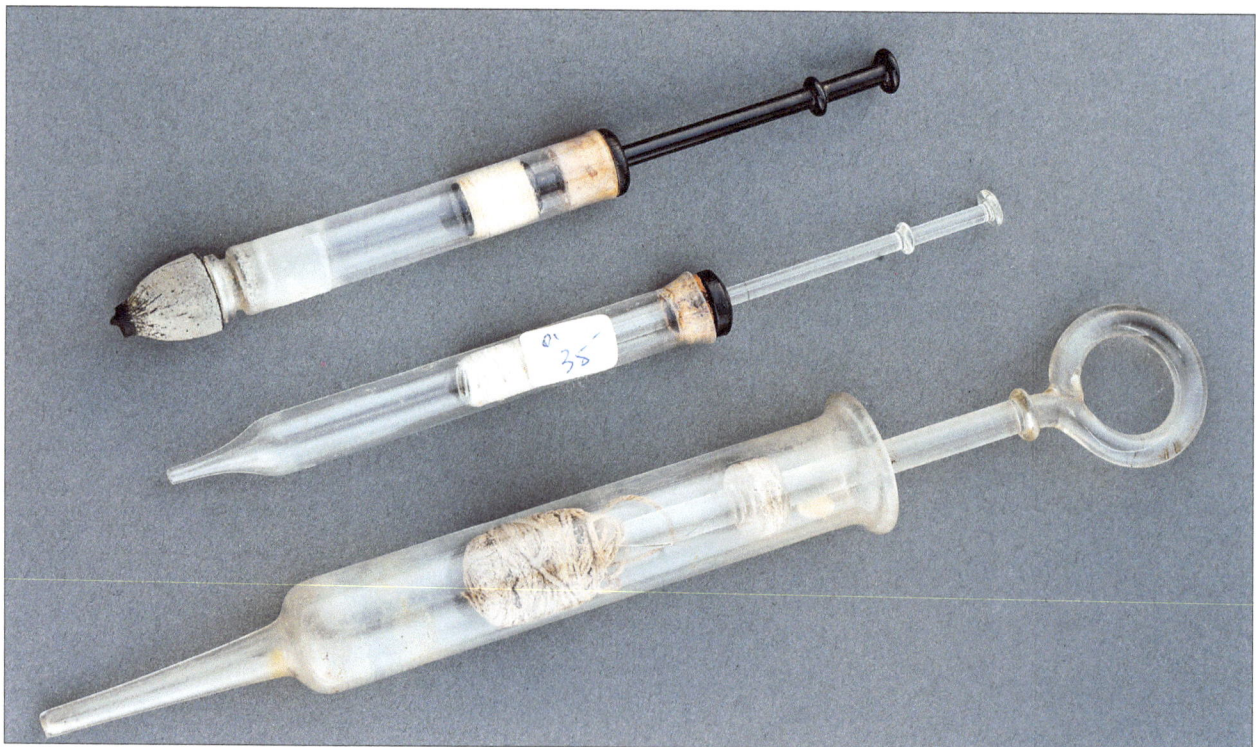

Glass syringes with thread plungers (early 19th century).

and then employing a hard-rubber syringe filled with water heated to 100° to dislodge impacted cerumen.[136]

The Touma ENT Museum houses a wide collection of ear syringes that illustrate the progression of materials used. The earliest examples have cylinders made of ivory and plungers made of wound thread. Another example has a pewter body with a thread plunger. Later syringes would be made of glass but retain the thread plungers. Speaking to the outdated nature of these syringes in 1853, Wilde dismisses them as "really of little or no use."[137] By this point

in the mid-19th century, the best syringes were those with rubber or cork plungers and stainless steel or brass cylinders. One example, made by Down Brothers of London, features a metal cylinder, ivory tip, and rubber plunger. A similar design by S. Man and Sons Ltd. differs only by a metal tip and another syringe by a metal plunger. Many of the brass and steel syringes were designed with loops at the back of the cylinder to allow the physician the dexterity of the fingers in handling them. These loops and varied materials made for instruments were both functional and decorative.

Ear syringes by different manufacturers. (Left) Down Brothers, London, with ivory cannula. (Middle) unlabeled. (Right) S. Man & Son Ltd., London.

Glass and steel syringe (early 20th century).

Wilde also describes a device that allowed patients to syringe their own ears, despite widespread concurrence that it should be avoided. This syringe, invented by Dr. S.P. Hullihen, a well-known dentist and surgeon from Wheeling, West Virginia, was housed in a small metal cup that could be placed next to the patient's ear. While holding the device, the patient could plunge the syringe, with the water and debris exiting the canal and draining into the metal cup.[138]

These examples are all simple mechanisms that require the drawing up of liquid through the tip of the syringe. An attachment developed by Becton Dickinson and Company can be placed on the end of a glass syringe, with an axillary outlet and an internal valve such that water can be drawn up through this additional outlet. With the valve then moved into the proper position, the axillary outlet is shut off and the syringe can then be used as normal. Another Becton Dickinson design operates via a two-way valve

and spring mechanism within the cylinder for the same purpose. Yet another interesting way to force water into the ear is seen with an ear irrigator that appears in an 1898 French medical supply catalogue called *Illustre des Instruments de Chirurgie* by the Parisian company Pelletier Aine. This irrigator relies on gravity to syphon water from a reservoir placed above the level of the patient's ear. The water runs through a piece of rubber tubing and into the ear via a speculum. The wash then exits via the same speculum and drains through another piece of tubing that runs into a collection basin set below the patient's ear.

Physicians have offered additional considerations with respect to cleaning the ear, meant to protect both themselves and their patients. Oren Pomeroy, for example, suggests in his textbook *The Diagnosis and Treatment of Diseases of the Ear* using a flange between the syringe tip and the rest of the cylinder to prevent backwash from getting on the physician.[139] Trying to

Rubber bulb and metal spoon-style ear syringe. Label on blub reads: "Sterilizable — Guaranteed English Made."

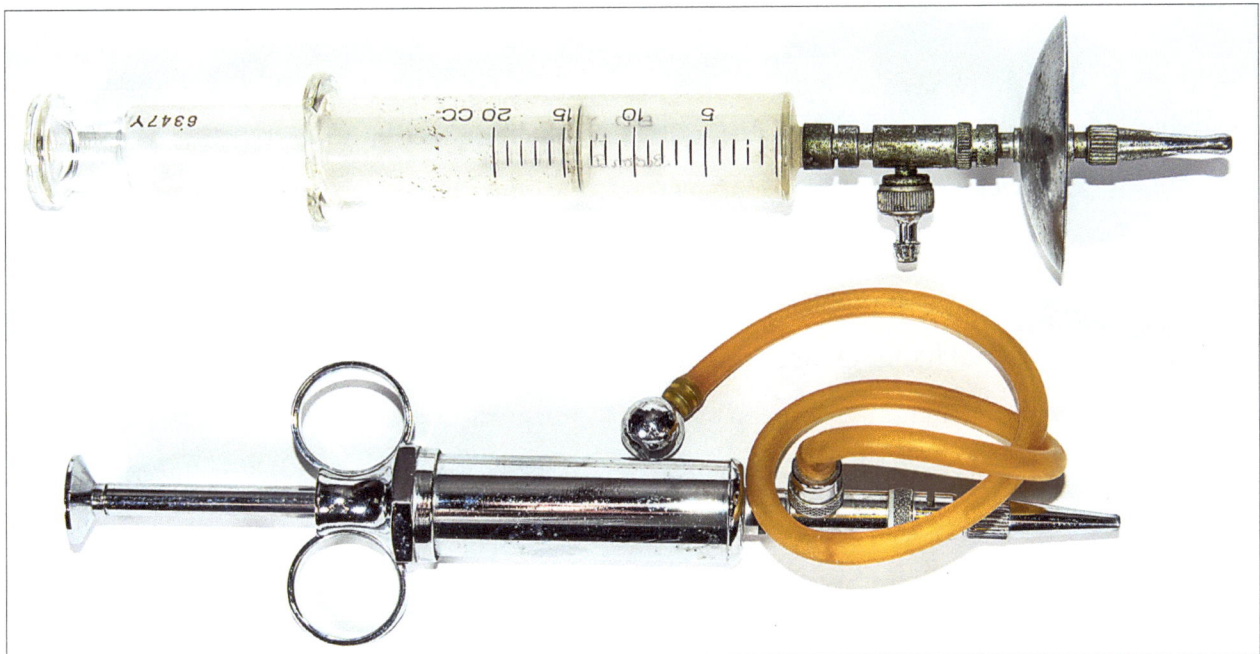

(Top) B-D Yale Leur-Lock glass ear syringe made by Becton Dickenson & Co. The valve in the spout allows for irrigant to be drawn into the syringe. (Bottom) Metal dual-valve syringe. The metal weight at the end of the tubing keeps it submerged.

(Top) Hosmer's ear spout with headband. (Bottom) Hosmer's ear loop could be placed around the patient's ear to collect irrigation drainage.

keep the patient's neck and shoulders clear of water and runoff proves a more difficult task. Many authors, including Wilde, suggest using a kidney basin, which fits nicely beside the head and neck of the patient — but this requires an additional hand, usually the patient's. Another instrument that has been used in the past is the ear spout. Toynbee advocates the ear spout as a "very serviceable" means of allowing drainage to run away from the patient and collect in a basin.[140] These ear spouts, as seen in the Touma collection and in Toynbee's illustrations, can be fixed in place by a simple loop around the patient's ear or a spring steel band across the crown of the patient's head.

The Touma collection contains many other interesting devices used to irrigate the ears. One inventor applied a spoon-shaped metal piece on one side of the rubber bulb for a more effective "squeeze" of the bulb. There are similar devices in the collection such as the B.D. Yale Leur-Lock glass ear syringe and a metal dual-valve ear syringe.

Various types of rubber bulbs have been popular for self-cleaning, such as the Ingram

Spring-loaded ear irrigation syringe (circa 1940s). The coil inside the narrow area compresses when the water is drawn and discharges it when released.

and the Boots bulbs. Another early 20th-century ear syringe is a glass syringe with metal ends, identical to the metal syringes.

A metal spring-loaded irrigation syringe is yet another unusual ear syringe. The water is drawn by pulling the plunger, which in turn compresses the coil; when the coil is released, the water is discharged from the cannula.

Left: Ingram's, London, rubber bulb. Right: Boots Cash Chemists rubber bulb.

Ear basin to catch water during ear irrigation.

OTOSCOPES with
SPECIAL ATTACHMENTS

Throughout the development of the otoscope special attachments using the same light source were invented. The most common attachment was the nasal speculum. Other attachments include pharyngoscopes, laryngoscopes and laryngeal mirrors.

There were several mechanisms to open the nasal speculum valves. Boehm's nasal speculum attachment has one arm that plugs into the light source. The light bulb with a condensing lens sat behind the speculum valves. Gowlland's nasal speculum attachment is a common speculum with a screw to open and close the valves. Welch Allyn otoscope has an unusual nasal speculum with a handle on one side. The speculum valves open by pulling the handle toward the body of the otoscope. The light bulb with condensing lens sits at the level of the valves. Keeler otoscope has a nasal speculum attachment with a lever below the speculum.

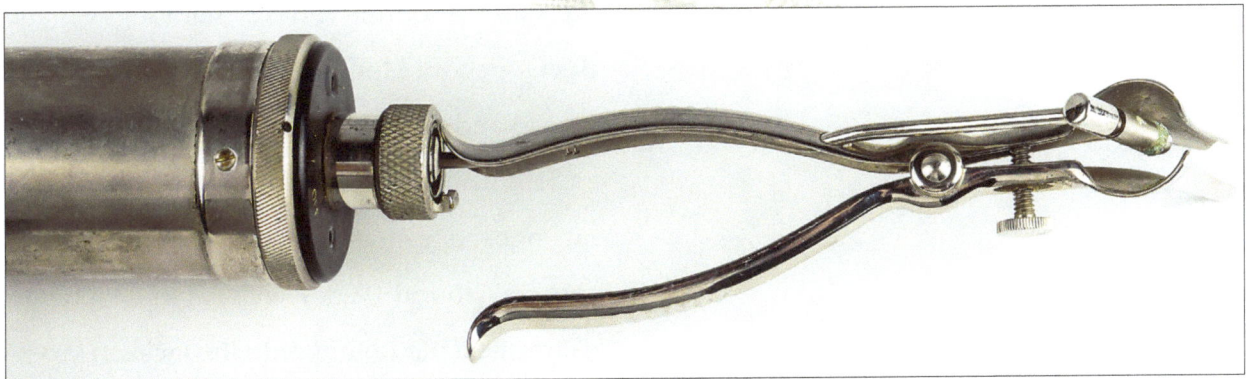

Boehm otoscope with nasal speculum attachment plugged into the light source.

The lever opens the valve when pulled toward the otoscope handle. While Welch Allyn's wire nasal speculum can be pressed together in order to insert it into the nose. Miller has a nasal speculum with an inscription "Patent Pending." It has a complex bi-valve plastic nasal speculum attachment. The valves open by clicking a ratcheting mechanism. They come back together by pushing a button situated on the side of the speculum.

Another popular attachment to the otoscope is the pharyngoscope attachment. As with nasal speculum attachments, there are many types.

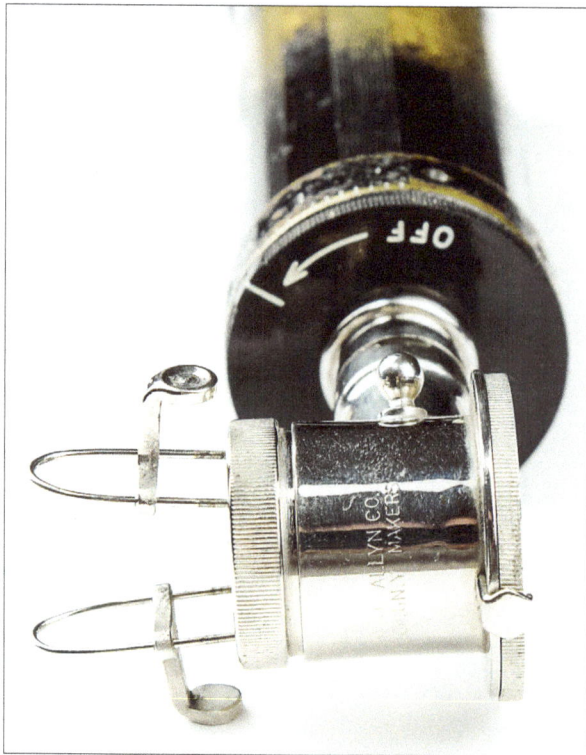

Miller surgical nasal speculum attachment with complex system to click valves open and a button to bring them back together (circa 1920s).

Welch Allyn wire nasal speculum attachment (circa 1920s). The wire valves can be compressed together by squeezing the protruding levers to introduce it to the nostril.

The Cameron otoscope has a plastic cannula that narrows toward the tip and opens from the top. Welch Allyn developed a closed metal cannula attachment similar to the Cameron otoscope. A routine half-circular tongue blade developed by Modell EEF D.R.R.CM. is open on top and attaches to the light source.

Still another interesting attachment is a laryngoscope that uses the otoscope's light source. Around 1920, Welch Allyn developed a laryngeal blade similar to the Jackson laryngoscope that enables the examiner to inspect

Otoscopes with different types of nasal specula: (from left to right) Gowlland, Otoscope, Wellch Allyn Otoscope, and Keeler Otoscope.

Various nasal specula attachments.

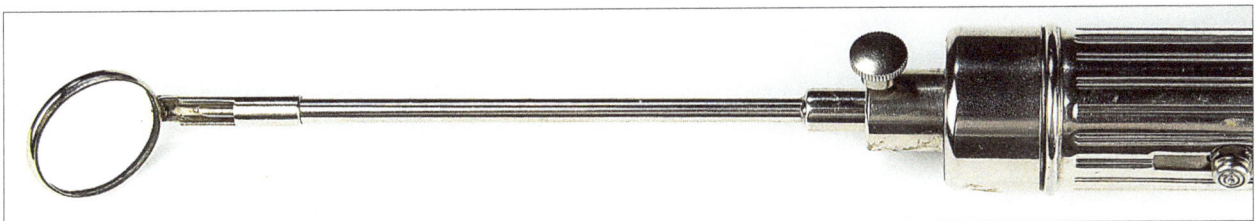

SASS. WOLF U Co. otoscope with laryngeal mirror attachment (circa 1930s).

the larynx. Several otoscope sets included laryngeal mirror attachments with a small light bulb close to the mirror.

In the 1960s, Welch Allyn developed a teaching otoscope with a side-view tube and pneumatic capabilities; interestingly, the 45° angle mirror concept was used by Brunton and Clarke 100 years earlier.

1920 Welch Allyn otoscope, Auburn, New York, with laryngoscoy attachment.

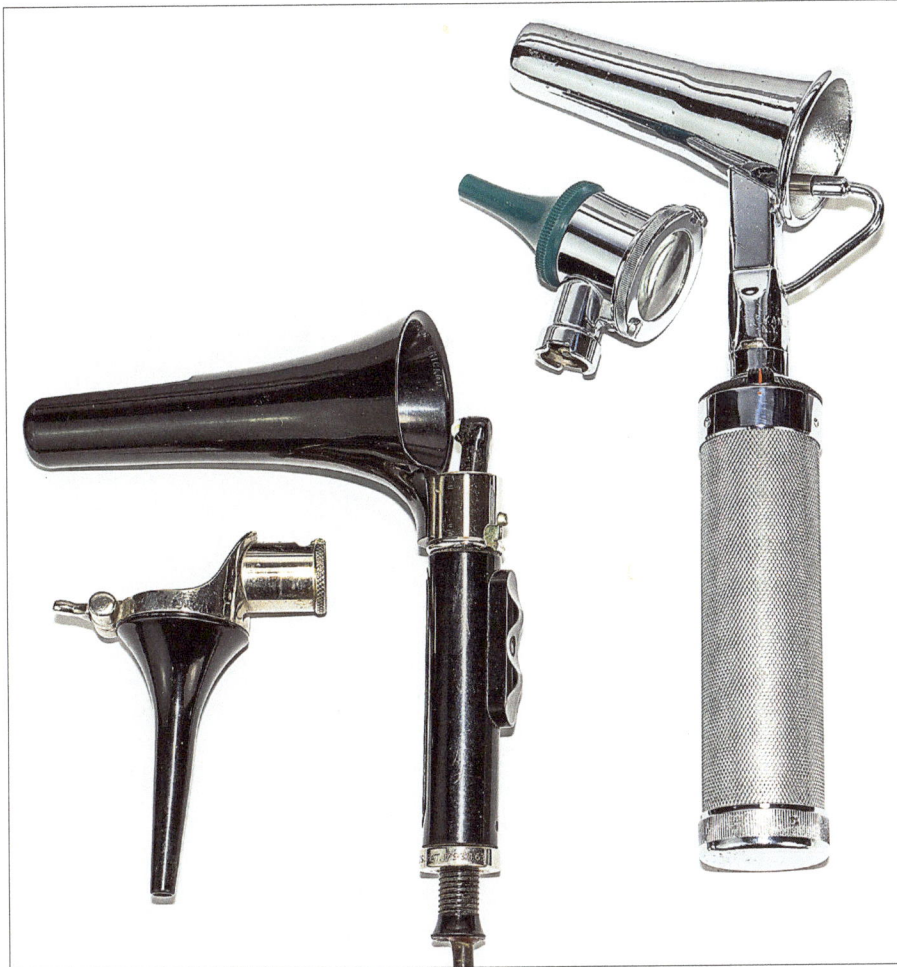

Pharyngoscopy attachments. (From left) Cameron otoscope, Welch Allyn otoscope.

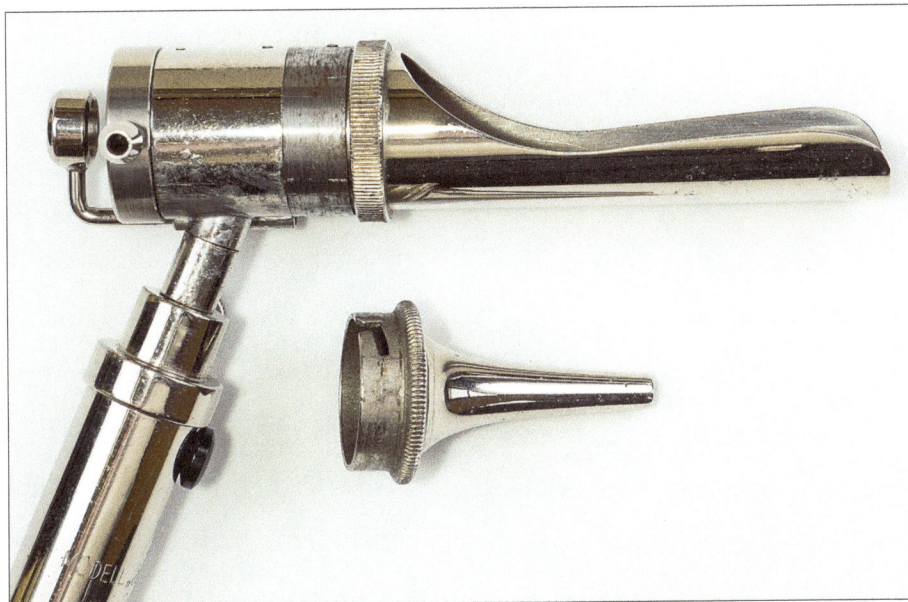

Otoscope "Modell EFF D.R.C.M." with tongue blade attachment.

PIONEERS in OTOLOGY and HISTORIC BOOKS

The illustrious history of otology would be nonexistent without the courage, imagination, sacrifice, ingenuity, and dedication of the pioneers whose names and contributions are mentioned in this book.

As early as the 18th century, the innovation of pioneers like Friedrich Hofmann — the first to use a perforated concave mirror to examine the ears — brought forth an explosion in the design and capabilities of the otoscope.

Guichard Joseph Du Verney published a monumental textbook on otology in Latin in 1730. His drawings of the anatomy of the ear and description of the ossicles and inner ear were very similar to the work of later anatomists who had the tools to make this study much easier and more complete.

In 1817, John Cunningham Saunders, a professor of practical anatomy at St. Thomas's Hospital in London, published a textbook, *Anatomy of the Human Ear*, with excellent demonstrations and pictures.

J.M. Gaspard Itard published the two-volume textbook *Treatise on Diseases of the Ear and Hearing* in French. It remained the standard textbook of otology for several decades.

Prosper Ménière, well known because of the syndrome that carries his name, was one of the early otologists who described Ménière's disease with accuracy. He authored many articles and published an otology textbook.

N.C. Deleau Jeune was Ménière's fellow Frenchman who was the first to use tubular speculum.

In the mid-19th century, Wilhelm Kramer was the most prominent otologist in Germany. He quickly gained the respect of other otologists throughout Europe. He was a pioneer in otoscopy and pre-electric lighting. Kramer's textbook *Aural Surgery of the Present Day* was translated into several languages, including English, and was taught at medical schools in Europe and the United States.

James Hinton was a noted otologist and a philosopher.

Sir William Wilde was another leading European otologist of the mid-19th century. His conical speculum was used widely in both pre-electric and post-electric otoscopes. Like his mother, Jane, and his son, Oscar, he was also a poet.

Jean Pierre Bonafont, a military surgeon was the first to develop the first single-piece otoscope.

Joseph Toynbee, considered the most respected pathological anatomist of the mid-19th century, dissected over 1,500 temporal bones. He was one of the earliest pioneers in understanding the surgical anatomy of the temporal bones.

Frederich Voltolini was known for his research and inventions.

In 1874, Professor Hermann von Helmholtz published a landmark book *The Mechanism of the Ossicles of the Ear and Membrana Tympani.*

The book included Professor Anton Von Tröltsch's, *Surgical Diseases of the Ear* textbook.

The far-reaching contributions of Adam Politzer, the most celebrated otologist, include authoring several textbooks and atlases that were translated into multiple languages, including English. Many otologists of his era visited him at the Institut für Geschichte der Universität Wien. In 1987, he was honored with the issuance of an Austrian postage stamp bearing his portrait.

In the late 19th century and early 20th century, Arthur Hartmann was Germany's leading otologist. He invented the first audiometer and many otological instruments, and his ear speculum is still in use in some otoscopes today.

The authors would be remiss not to mention Hans Key-Aberg, who in 1919 published *Historical Review of Instruments Used in Otoscopy, Together with a Description of a Method for Photographing the Membrana Tympani.* No other textbook on the history of otoscopy has been published since.

The Viennese otologist Joseph Gruber invented the widely used ear speculum that could be found in medical catalogues as late as the 1950s.

Johannes Luae, a leading German otologist, developed an ear speculum with oblique tips.

FRIEDRICH HOFFMAN (1660-1742). Hoffman invented his own speculum and was the first to use a centrally perforated concave mirror. He was a general practitioner in Burgsteinfurt, Germany

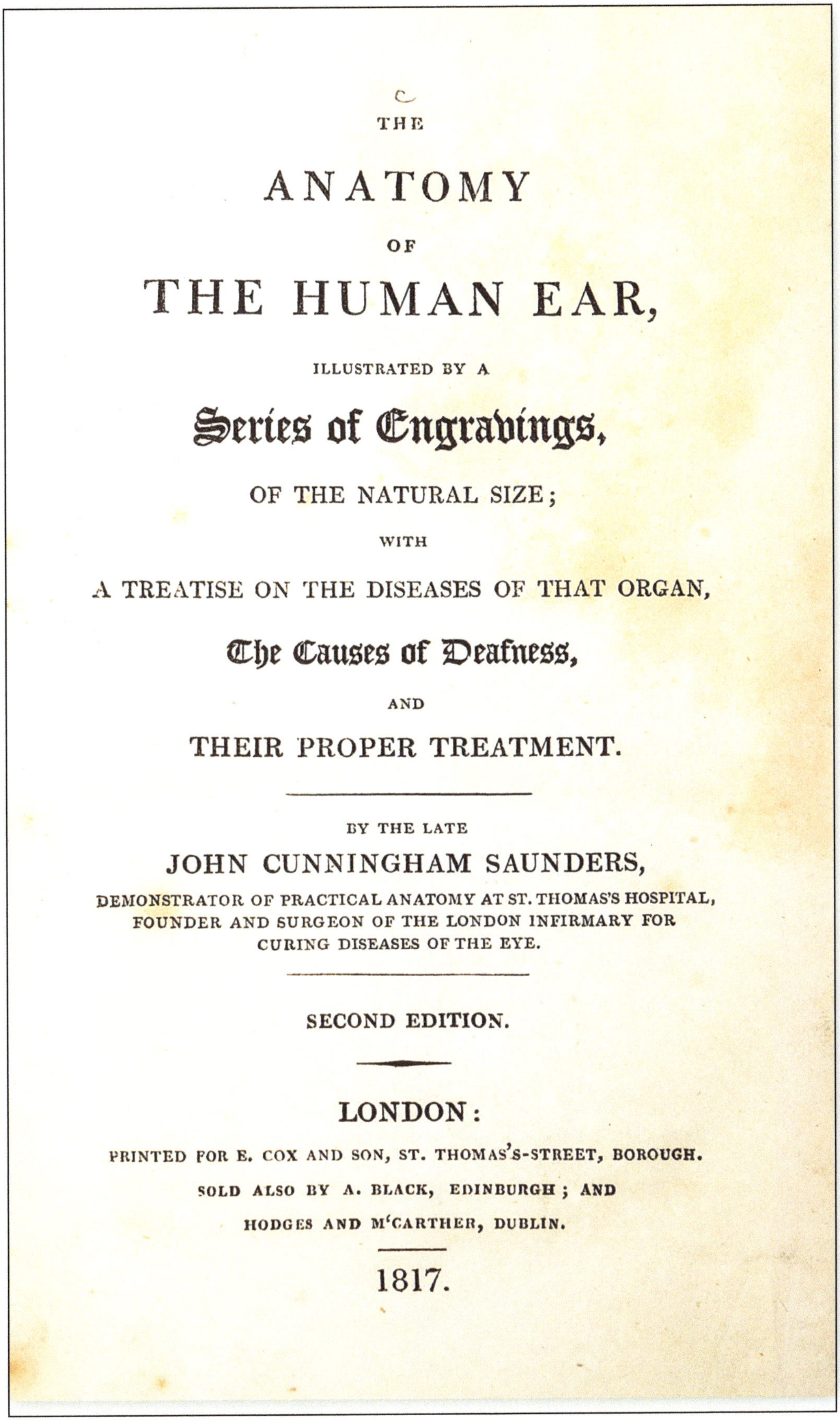

THE

ANATOMY

OF

THE HUMAN EAR,

ILLUSTRATED BY A

Series of Engravings,

OF THE NATURAL SIZE;

WITH

A TREATISE ON THE DISEASES OF THAT ORGAN,

The Causes of Deafness,

AND

THEIR PROPER TREATMENT.

BY THE LATE

JOHN CUNNINGHAM SAUNDERS,

DEMONSTRATOR OF PRACTICAL ANATOMY AT ST. THOMAS'S HOSPITAL,
FOUNDER AND SURGEON OF THE LONDON INFIRMARY FOR
CURING DISEASES OF THE EYE.

SECOND EDITION.

LONDON:

PRINTED FOR E. COX AND SON, ST. THOMAS'S-STREET, BOROUGH.

SOLD ALSO BY A. BLACK, EDINBURGH; AND

HODGES AND M'CARTHER, DUBLIN.

1817.

J.M. GASPARD ITARD (1774-1838). Itard was pioneer in treating the deaf and mute and the author of *Treatise on the Diseases of the Ear and Hearing*, a comprehensive two-volume early textbook on otology.

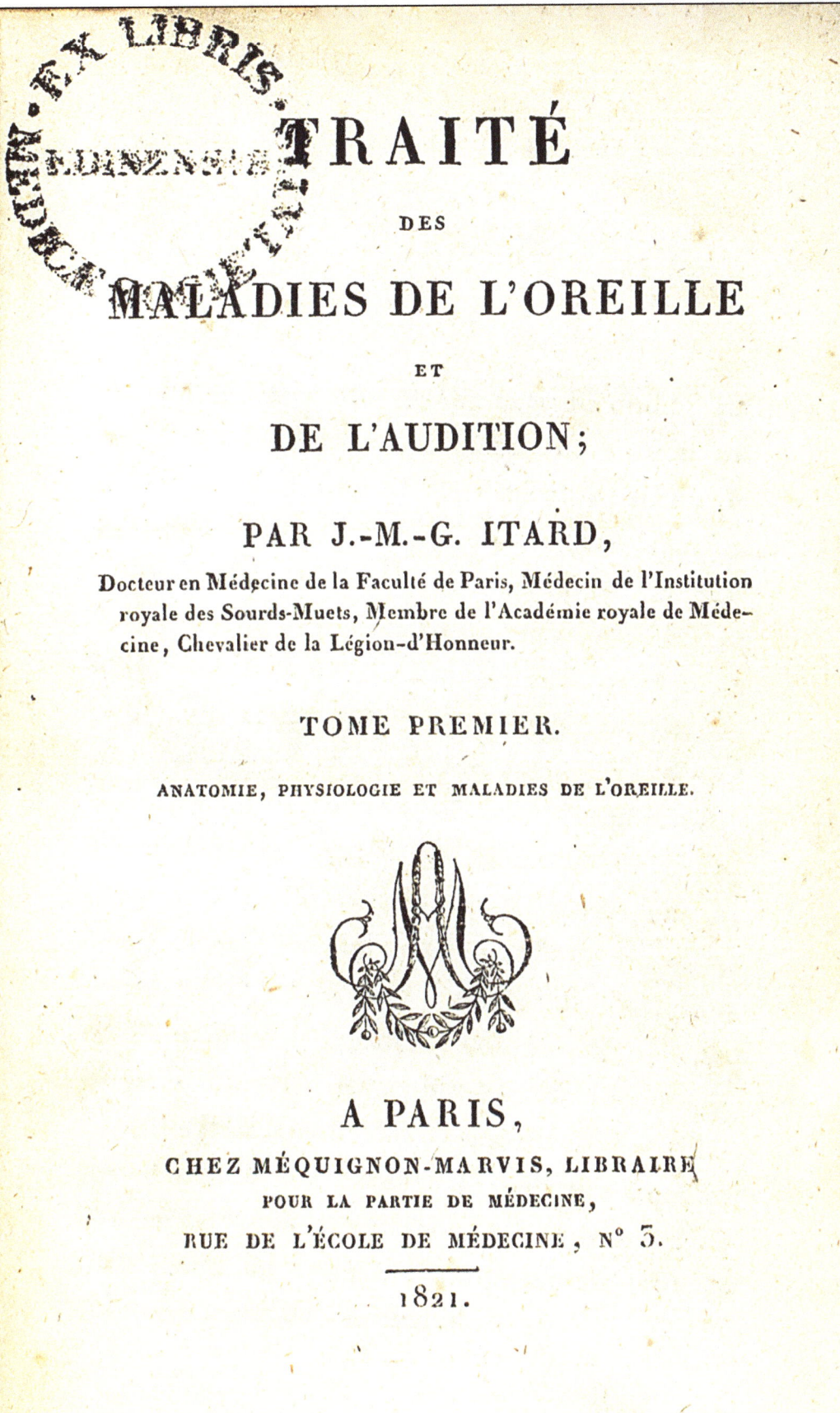

TRAITÉ

DES

MALADIES DE L'OREILLE

ET

DE L'AUDITION;

PAR J.-M.-G. ITARD,

Docteur en Médecine de la Faculté de Paris, Médecin de l'Institution royale des Sourds-Muets, Membre de l'Académie royale de Médecine, Chevalier de la Légion-d'Honneur.

TOME PREMIER.

ANATOMIE, PHYSIOLOGIE ET MALADIES DE L'OREILLE.

A PARIS,

CHEZ MÉQUIGNON-MARVIS, LIBRAIRE

POUR LA PARTIE DE MÉDECINE,

RUE DE L'ÉCOLE DE MÉDECINE, N° 3.

1821.

TRACTATUS
DE
ORGANO
AUDITUS.

CONTINENS STRUCTURAM, USUM, ET MORBOS OMNIUM AURIS PARTIUM

Authore

DN. DU VERNEY,

Academiæ Scientiarum Regiæ Socio, Consiliario & Medico Ordinario Regis, Professore Anatomiæ & Chirurgiæ in Horto Regio Plantarum.

E Gallico Latinè redditus.

VERSIO NOVA ET ACCURATIOR.

LUGDUNI BATAVORUM,

Apud JOH: ARNOLD: LANGERAK,

MDCCXXX.

HISTORICAL REVIEW OF INSTRUMENTS USED IN OTOSCOPY,

TOGETHER WITH

A DESCRIPTION OF A METHOD FOR PHOTO-GRAPHING THE MEMBRANA TYMPANI

BY

HANS KEY-ÅBERG

STOCKHOLM 1919

KUNGL. BOKTRYCKERIET. P. A. NORSTEDT & SÖNER

190288

PROSPER MÉNIÈRE (1799-1862). Ménière was one of the giants of early otology. He was the first to describe the disease that carries his name.

TRAITÉ

DES

MALADIES DE L'OREILLE

PAR LE DOCTEUR

GUILL. KRAMER,

MÉDECIN PRATICIEN A BERLIN.

Traduit de l'allemand,

AVEC DES NOTES ET DES ADDITIONS NOMBREUSES,

PAR LE DOCTEUR

P. MENIÈRE,

Médecin de l'institution royale des sourds-muets de Paris,
agrégé de la Faculté de médecine, etc., etc.

———————

Cinq figures intercalées dans le texte.

———◦———

PARIS.

GERMER BAILLIÈRE, LIBRAIRE-ÉDITEUR,

RUE DE L'ÉCOLE-DE-MÉDECINE, 17.

A LONDRES,
Chez H. Baillière, 219, Regent-Street.
A LEIPZIG,
Chez Brockhaus et Avenarius, Michelsen.
A SAINT-PÉTERSBOURG,
Chez Issakoff.

A MONTPELLIER,
Chez Castel, Sevalle.
A LYON,
Chez Savy, 14, place Louis-le-Grand.
A FLORENCE,
Chez Ricordi et Jouaud.

1848.

NIC. DELEAU JEUNE (1799-1862). Deleau, a French otologist often overshadowed by his fellow countrymen Itard and Ménière, invented two illumination devices for inspecting the ear and was the first to use a tubular speculum.

TRAITÉ

DU

CATHÉTÉRISME

DE LA TROMPE D'EUSTACHI,

ET DE L'EMPLOI DE L'AIR ATMOSPHÉRIQUE

DANS LES MALADIES DE L'OREILLE MOYENNE.

PAR LE Dʳ DELEAU Jeune.

« Des difficultés apparentes ne doivent pas faire renoucer
aux entreprises utiles ; il faut, au contraire, s'imposer la loi de
cette persévérance qui rend l'homme capable de tout ce qui est
bien, surtout quand il s'agit des choses sur lesquelles repose
souvent la base de l'existence et de la conservation. »

(POLYBE, lib. X, chap. 44.)

PARIS.

GERMER-BAILLIÈRE, RUE DE L'ÉCOLE DE MÉDECINE, 17 ;
L'AUTEUR, RUE DE SEINE-SAINT-GERMAIN, 6.

1838.

WILHELM KRAMER (1801-1875). Kramer was one of the most prominent otologists of his time. His philosophy of symptomatology shaped the German schooling for much of the mid-19th century. He was also well known for his speculum and ear lamp.

THE

AURAL SURGERY

OF THE PRESENT DAY.

BY

DR. W. KRAMER,

BERLIN.

WITH TWO TABLES AND NINE WOODCUTS.

TRANSLATED BY

HENRY POWER, ESQ., F.R.C.S., M.B. LOND.,

ASSISTANT-SURGEON AND LECTURER ON PHYSIOLOGY AT THE WESTMINSTER HOSPITAL, AN
SURGEON TO THE ROYAL WESTMINSTER OPHTHALMIC HOSPITAL.

WITH CORRECTIONS AND NUMEROUS ADDITIONS
BY THE AUTHOR.

THE NEW SYDENHAM SOCIETY,
LONDON.

MDCCCLXIII.

JAMES HINTON (1822-1875). Hinton made worthy contributions to otology, incuding a demonstration otoscope. While a well-recognized physician, he is known better as a philospher.

JEAN PIERRE BONNAFONT (1805-1891). Bonnafont was a French military surgeon who contributed significantly to otology. He developed the first single-piece otoscope, predating Brunton's by three decades.

SIR WILLIAM WILDE (1815-1876). Wilde was one of Europe's leading otologists. His contribution to otoscopy was the invention of a conical speculum. Married to Irish poetess Speranza. Their son Oscar Wilde obviously followed in his mother's footsteps, becoming a famed poet himself.

PRACTICAL OBSERVATIONS

ON

AURAL SURGERY

AND

THE NATURE AND TREATMENT

OF

DISEASES OF THE EAR.

With Illustrations.

BY

WILLIAM R. WILDE,

FELLOW OF THE ROYAL COLLEGE OF SURGEONS IN IRELAND; SURGEON TO ST. MARK'S OPHTHALMIC
HOSPITAL; HONORARY MEMBER OF THE ROYAL MEDICAL SOCIETY OF STOCKHOLM, ETC., ETC.

PHILADELPHIA:
BLANCHARD & LEA.
1853.

JOSEPH TOYNBEE (1815-1866). Toynbee is considered the father of British otology and one of the most respected pathologic anatomists. He is famed for many accomplishments including over 1,500 temporal bone dissections.

THE

DISEASES OF THE EAR:

THEIR

NATURE, DIAGNOSIS, AND TREATMENT.

BY

JOSEPH TOYNBEE, F.R.S.

FELLOW OF THE ROYAL COLLEGE OF SURGEONS OF ENGLAND;
AURAL SURGEON TO, AND LECTURER ON AURAL SURGERY AT, ST. MARY'S HOSPITAL;
AURAL SURGEON TO THE ASYLUM FOR IDIOTS;
CONSULTING AURAL SURGEON TO THE ASYLUM FOR THE DEAF AND DUMB;
AND CONSULTING SURGEON
TO THE ST. GEORGE'S AND ST. JAMES'S GENERAL DISPENSARY, LONDON.

LONDON:
JOHN CHURCHILL, NEW BURLINGTON STREET.
MDCCCLX.

FREDERICK VOLTOLINI (1819-1899). Voltolini made several contributions to otoscopy. As Dozent of Otology and Laryngology at Breslau, his research focused on the hearing organs.

THE SURGICAL DISEASES

OF

THE EAR.

BY

PROF. VON TRÖLTSCH.

THE

MECHANISM OF THE OSSICLES

AND

THE MEMBRANA TYMPANI.

BY

PROF. HELMHOLTZ.

TRANSLATED FROM THE GERMAN

BY

JAMES HINTON.

THE NEW SYDENHAM SOCIETY

LONDON.

MDCCCLXXIV.

ADAM POLITZER (1835-1920). Politzer's contributions to the field of otology are far reaching. He invented diagnostic and therapeutic devices and authored textbooks and atlases. He spent his career at the Institut fur Geschichte der Universitat, Wien.

LEHRBUCH

DER

OHRENHEILKUNDE

FÜR

PRACTISCHE ÄRZTE UND STUDIRENDE

VON

DR. ADAM POLITZER,

K. K. ORD. ÖFFENT. PROFESSOR DER OHRENHEILKUNDE AN DER WIENER UNIVERSITÄT,
VORSTAND DER K. K. UNIVERSITÄTS-KLINIK FÜR OHRENKRANKE IM ALLGEMEINEN KRANKENHAUSE,
K. K. ARMEN-OHRENARZT DER STADT WIEN.

Vierte gänzlich umgearbeitete Auflage.

MIT 346 IN DEN TEXT GEDRUCKTEN ABBILDUNGEN.

STUTTGART.
VERLAG VON FERDINAND ENKE.
1901.

ATLAS AND EPITOME

OF

OTOLOGY

BY

GUSTAV BRÜHL, M. D.

of Berlin

WITH THE COLLABORATION OF

PROF. DR. A. POLITZER

of Vienna

AUTHORIZED TRANSLATION FROM THE GERMAN

EDITED BY

S. MacCUEN SMITH, M. D.

Clinical Professor of Otology, Jefferson Medical College, Philadelphia;
Otologist and Laryngologist to the Germantown
Hospital, Philadelphia

With 244 Colored Figures on 39 Lithographic Plates, and 99
Text Illustrations

PHILADELPHIA AND LONDON

W. B. SAUNDERS & COMPANY

1902

A TEXT-BOOK

OF THE

DISEASES OF THE EAR

FOR STUDENTS AND PRACTITIONERS

BY

PROFESSOR DR. ADAM POLITZER

IMPERIAL-ROYAL PROFESSOR OF AURAL THERAPEUTICS IN THE UNIVERSITY OF VIENNA;
CHIEF OF THE IMPERIAL-ROYAL UNIVERSITY CLINIC FOR DISEASES OF THE
EAR IN THE GENERAL HOSPITAL, VIENNA, ETC.

TRANSLATED AT THE PERSONAL REQUEST OF THE AUTHOR, AND
EDITED BY

MILTON J. BALLIN, Ph.B., M.D.

ASSISTANT SURGEON, NEW YORK OPHTHALMIC AND AURAL INSTITUTE; ASSISTANT SURGEON,
MOUNT SINAI DISPENSARY, EAR, NOSE AND THROAT DEPARTMENT; ETC.

AND

CLARENCE L. HELLER, M.D.

FIFTH EDITION, REVISED AND ENLARGED
WITH 337 ORIGINAL ILLUSTRATIONS

LEA & FEBIGER
PHILADELPHIA AND NEW YORK
1909

ARTHUR HARTMANN (1849-1931). Hartmann was a highly regarded German otologist. He invented a widely used speculum, the first audiometer and several iinstruments and devices.

THE

DISEASES OF THE EAR

AND THEIR TREATMENT.

BY

ARTHUR HARTMANN, M.D.,

BERLIN.

TRANSLATED FROM THE THIRD GERMAN EDITION BY

JAMES ERSKINE, M.A., M.B.,

SURGEON FOR DISEASES OF THE EAR TO ANDERSON'S COLLEGE DISPENSARY,
GLASGOW ; LATE ASSISTANT-SURGEON TO THE GLASGOW HOSPITAL
AND DISPENSARY FOR DISEASES OF THE EAR.

WITH FORTY-TWO ILLUSTRATIONS.

EDINBURGH:
YOUNG J. PENTLAND.
1887.

JOSEF GRUBER (1827-1900). Gruber was on faculty at the University of Vienna. He invented a popular speculum design.

A TEXT-BOOK

OF THE

DISEASES OF THE EAR

BY

DR. JOSEF GRUBER

PROFESSOR OF OTOLOGY IN THE IMPERIAL ROYAL UNIVERSITY OF VIENNA, ETC.

TRANSLATED FROM THE SECOND GERMAN EDITION BY SPECIAL PERMISSION OF THE AUTHOR

AND EDITED BY

EDWARD LAW, M.D., C.M. Edin., M.R.C.S. Eng.

SURGEON TO THE LONDON THROAT HOSPITAL FOR DISEASES OF THE THROAT, NOSE AND EAR

AND BY

COLEMAN JEWELL, M.B. Lond., M.R.C.S. Eng.

LATE PHYSICIAN AND PATHOLOGIST TO THE LONDON THROAT HOSPITAL

WITH 150 ILLUSTRATIONS AND 70 COLOURED FIGURES ON 2 LITHOGRAPHIC PLATES

NEW YORK

D. APPLETON & CO., 1, 3 & 5, BOND STREET

1891

JOHANNES LUCAE (1835-1911). Lucae was a dozent and honorary professor at the University of Berlin and one of the leading German otologists. Lucae made several contributions to otology, notably an obliquely sectioned speculum and a demonstration otoscope.

FOOTNOTES

1. Politzer A. *History of Otology*. Translated by Stanley Milstein, et al. Phoenix, AZ: Columnella Press; 1981, 219.
2. Willemot, et al. 417.
3. Op. cit. #1. 32.
4. Wilde W. Some Observations on the Early History of Aural Surgery, and the Nosological Arrangement of Diseases of the Ear. *Dublin Journal of Medical Science*. 1844; 25: 426.
5. Op. cit. #1. 88-90.
6. Key-Aberg H. *Historical Review of Instruments Used in Otoscopy, Together with a Description of a Method for Photographing the Membrana Tympani*. Stockholm, Sweden: P.A. Norstedt & Söner; 1919, 25.
7. Op. cit. #6. 27.
8. Op. cit. #6. 28.
9. Op. cit. #1. 293.
10. Op. cit. #1. 291.
11. Touma J. Prosper Ménière: A glimpse at his personality and time from his introduction of Kramer's book, "Diseases of the Ear." *The American Journal of Otology*. 1986; 7: 307.
12. Op. cit. #1. 297.
13. Op. cit. #6. 28-29.
14. Nezhat C. *Nezhat's History of Endoscopy*. Tuttlingen, Germany: Endo Press; 2011, 33.
15. Op. cit. #6. 36.
16. Op. cit. #6. 31.
17. Op. cit. #6. 36.
18. Op. cit. #6. 26.
19. Feldmann H. History of the ear speculum. *Laryngorhinootologie*. 1996; 75(5): 311-318.
20. Op. cit. #6. 31.
21. Politzer A. *A Text-book of Diseases of the Ear*. Translated by Milton Ballin and Clarence Heller. New York, NY: Lea and Febiger: 1909, 97.
22. Wilde W. Upon the Causes and Treatment of Otorrhea. *Dublin Journal of Medical Science*. 1844; 24: 394.
23. Wilde W. *Practical Observations on Aural Surgery and the Nature and Treatment of Diseases of the Ear*. Philadelphia, PA: Blanchard and Lea; 1853, 72.
24. Toynbee J. On a new ear speculum. *Lancet*. 1850; 56: 391.
25. Op. cit. #6. 34.
26. Mudry A. The Role of Adam Politzer (1835-1920) in the History of Otology. *The American Journal of Otology*. 2000; 21: 757.
27. Op. cit. #19.
28. Op. cit. #24. 753-758.
29. Op. cit. #6. 34.
30. Op. cit. #6. 35.
31. Op. cit. #17.
32. Pappas D, Kent L. *Otology's Great Moments*. Birmingham, AL: Dennis Pappas; 2000, 113.
33. Op. cit. #6. 35.
34. Roosa D. *A Practical Treatise on the Diseases of the Ear, Including the Anatomy of the Organ*. New York, NY: William Wood & Company; 1873, 87.
35. Dolebear A. Edward Samuel Ritchie. *Proceedings of the American Academy of Arts and Sciences*. 1896; 23: 359-360.
36. Op. cit. #32.
37. Gruber J. *A Text-book of the Diseases of the Ear*. 2nd German Ed. Translated by Edward Law and Coleman Jewell. 2nd American Ed. New York, NY: D Appleton and Co; 1893, 166.
38. Op. cit. #30. 123.
39. Op. cit. #30. 42.
40. Op. cit. #6. 36-37.
41. Maloney J. Speculum. U.S. Patent 411,160, September 17, 1889.
42. Op. cit. #1. 68.
43. Op. cit. #1. 53.
44. Cleland A. A Description of Needles Made for Operations on the Eyes, and of Some Instruments for the Ears, by the Same. *Philosophical Transactions*. 1739; 41: 847-851.
45. Op. cit. #6. 3.
46. Op. cit. #6. 4.
47. Ibid.
48. Op. cit. #1. 284.
49. Op. cit. #6. 6.
50. Op. cit. #1. 276.
51. Op. cit. #20. 393.
52. Roggenkamp W. Der Ohrenspiegel. ?[this is an excerpt from a book *The History of the Medical Science of the Throat, Nose and Ear*, 649.
53. Op. cit. #20. 395.
54. Op. cit. #6. 10.
55. Op. cit. #50. 650-651.
56. Op. cit. #50. 652.
57. Op. cit. #50. 651.
58. Von Tröltsch A. *Treatise on Diseases of the Ear*. Translated by Daniel Roosa. New York: William Wood and Company; 1869, 71.
59. Weir N. *Otolaryngology: An Illustrated History*. London: Butterworth; 1990, 80.

60. Op. cit. #6. 14.
61. Ibid.
62. Foltz K. *Diseases of the Nose, Throat and Ear*. Cincinnati, OH: Scudder Brothers; 1906, 79.
63. Op. cit. #6. 9.
64. Op. cit. #59. 112.
65. Op. cit. #21. 70.
66. Op. cit. #50.
67. Toynbee J. *Diseases of the Ear*. Philadelphia, PA: Blanchard and Lea; 1860, 62-63.
68. Bacon G. *A Manual of Otology*. New York, NY: Lea Brothers; 1913, 69.
69. Op. cit. #62. 77.
70. Pomeroy O. *The Diagnosis and Treatment of Diseases of the Ear*. New York, NY: Bermingham; 1883, 122.
71. Kerrison P. *Diseases of the Ear*. Philadelphia, PA: J.B. Lippincott; 1913, 46.
72. Dench E. *Diseases of the Ear*. New York, NY: D. Appleton; 1904, 77.
73. Burnett C, Ingals E, Newcomb J. *A Text-book on Diseases of the Ear, Nose and Throat*. Philadelphia, PA: J.B. Lippincott; 1901, 76.
74. Op. cit. #71. 50.
75. Reinhard M, Eberhardt E. Alfred Kirstein (1863-1922)-pioneer in direct laryngoscopy. *Anasthesiol Intensivmed Notfallmed Schmerzther*. 1995; 30: 240.
76. Op. cit. #59. 246.
77. Phillips W. *Diseases of the Ear, Nose and Throat*. Philadelphia, PA: F.A. Davis; 1927, 4.
78. Wallace F. Surgical headlight and light source. U.S. Patent 3,285,242, November 15, 1966.
79. Politzer A. *Text-book of Diseases of the Ear and Adjacent Organs*. Translated by James Cassells. London: Balliere, Tindall and Cox; 1883, 93-34.
80. Op. cit. #19. 98.
81. Gross S. *A System of Surgery; Pathological, Diagnostic, Therapeutic and Operative*. Philadelphia, PA: Henry C. Lea; 1866, 300.
82. Jones H. *A Treatise on Aural Surgery*. London: J. & A. Churchill; 1881, 105-106.
83. Op. cit. #82. 108.
84. Op. cit. #19. 99.
85. Op. cit. #79. 93.
86. Op. cit. #6. 39.
87. Burnett C. *The Ear; Its Anatomy, Physiology and Diseases*. Philadelphia, PA: Henry C. Lea; 1877, 169.
88. Burnett C. Report on the Progress of Otology. *Boston Medical and Surgical Journal*. 1874; 90: 287.
89. Winslow W. *The Human Ear and its Diseases*. Philadelphia, PA: Boericke & Tafel; 1882, 87.
90. Keeler J, Clarence J. *Modern Otology*. Philadelphia, PA: F.A. Davis; 1930, 93.
91. Houghton H. *Lecture on Clinical Otology*. Boston, MA: Otis Clapp and Son; 1888, 11.
92. Schwartze H. *Die Chirurgischen Krankheiten des Ohres*. Stuttgart, Germany: Verlag von Ferdinand Enke; 1885, 9-10.
93. Op. cit. #30. 108.
94. Burnett C, Ingals E, Newcomb J. *A Text-book on Diseases of the Ear, Nose and Throat*. Philadelphia, PA: J.B. Lippincott; 1901, 78.
95. Packard F. *Text-book of Disease of the Nose, Throat and Ear*. Philadelphia, PA: Lippincott; 1909, 16.
96. Tod H. *Diseases of the Ear*. London: Oxford University Press; 1907, 110.
97. Op. cit. #68. 79.
98. Op. cit. #59. 154.
99. Love J. *Diseases of the Ear*. New York, NY: William Wood; 1905, 95.
100. Coleman W. *Electricity in Diseases of the Eye, Ear, Nose and Throat*. Chicago, IL: Courier-Herald Press; 1912, 414.
101. Op. cit. #19. 150.
102. Op. cit. #6. 12.
103. Op. cit. #2. 604.
104. Op. cit. #6. 17.
105. Op. cit. #59. 64.
106. Op. cit. #89. 83.
107. Clark J. The Reflecting Otoscope and Artificial Drum. *Medical and Surgical Reporter*. 1857; 10: 488.
108. Turnbull L. *A Clinical Manual of the Diseases of the Ear*. Philadelphia, PA: J.B. Lippincott; 1887, 65-66.
109. Op. cit. #6. 17.
110. Brunton J. A new otoscope or speculum auris. *Lancet*. 1865; 86: 617-618.
111. Op. cit. #59. 64-65.
112. Op. cit. #110.
113. Op. cit. #6. 19.
114. Brunton J. Dr. Brunton's otoscope. *The Medical Times and Gazette*. 1868; 1: 138.
115. Op. cit. #6. 18-19.
116. Op. cit. #6. 22.
117. Gruber J. *A Text-book of the Diseases of the Ear*. 2nd German Ed. Translated by Edward Law and Coleman Jewell. 2nd American Ed. New York, NY: D Appleton and Co; 1893, 166.
118. Hovell T. *A Treatise on Diseases of the Ear*. Philadelphia, PA: P. Blakiston; 1901, 83.
119. Op. cit. #79. 95.
120. Op. cit. #87. 170.
121. Vilardell F. *Digestive Endoscopy in the Second Millennium*. Stuttgart, Germany: Thieme; 2006, 88.
122. Barr T. *Manual of the Diseases of the Ear*. Glasgow, Scotland: James Maclehose and Sons; 1896, 9.
123. Op. cit. #59. 65.
124. Op. cit. #68. 63-64.
125. Patterson W. Otoscope. U.S. Patent 1,896,720, February 7, 1933.
126. Op. cit. #90. 94-95.
127. Cameron W. Illuminated telescope for instruments. U.S. Patent 1,896,861, February 7, 1933.
128. http://www.cameronville.com/crofts/tom-kari/cameron/bio-wjc.html
129. Cameron W. Handle for instruments for making examinations. U.S. Patent 1,793,463, February 24, 1931.
130. Dittmer A. Otoscope. U.S. Patent 2,184,414, December 26, 1939.
131. Brown A. Surgical and diagnostic instrument. U.S. Patent 2,235,979, March 25, 1941.
132. Moore W., et al. Illuminating means for medical instruments. U.S. Patent 3,146,775, September 1, 1964.
133. Moore W., et al. Otoscope construction. U.S. Patent 4,006,738, February 8, 1977.
134. Hotchkiss J. Endoscope with coincident illumination and viewing. U.S. Patent 3,596,653, August 3, 1971.
135. Op. cit. #21. 84.
136. Buck A. *First Principles of Otology*. New York, NY: William Wood and Company; 1899, 11-14.
137. Op. cit. #21. 85.
138. Ibid.
139. Pomeroy O. *The Diagnosis and Treatment of Diseases of the Ear*. 2nd Ed. New York, NY: Bermingham; 1886, 95.
140. Op. cit. #67. 84.